POSTGRADUATE STUDY

AT THE UNIVERSITY OF ST ANDREWS

St Andrews is the oldest univer- in Scotland, being founded in 1410. The University provides an invigorating intellectual climate in which staff have close contacts with one another and with colleagues in other U.K. and overseas universities and research establishments. All schools are actively involved in pushing back the frontiers of knowledge in both the sciences and the arts. A student population of approximately 5,900 allows its members a close sense of identity and personal contact with staff.

◆ School of Art History

The School has an international reputation for excellence in teaching/research, and its scholars/students number over 50. As the largest department of Art History in Scotland, it offers supervision in a wide range of areas, including ancient numismatics; mediaeval and Renaissance Italy; east European and Russian art and design; furniture history; Dada and Surrealism; C19th and C20th photography; Scottish art and architecture; museum/gallery studies. Degrees: Diploma, M.Litt., M.Phil., and Ph.D. in Art History; Diploma and M.Phil. in Museum/Gallery Studies; M.Phil. in National Trust for Scotland Studies.

◆ School of Biological and Medical Sciences

The School has active research groups in the following areas: Environmental Physiology, Evolutionary Relationships, Fish Biology, Marine Ecology, Plant Genetics, Plants/Molecular Biology and Animal Behaviour, Molecular Virology, Microbial Physiology, Neurosciences, Molecular Endocrinology, Cancer Biology, Cell and Developmental Biology and Biophysics. The School offers M.Phil. (2 years) and Ph.D. (3 years) research degrees in all these areas. Further details available from: Dr. Neil Hazon, Postgraduate Admissions, School of Biological Sciences, University of St Andrews, St Andrews, Fife, KY16 8LB UK.

◆ School of English

The School of English runs M.Litt. courses in Mediaeval English, Scottish Literature, Shakespeare Studies and Creative Writing. Research and funding opportunities at Ph.D. and M.Phil. level exist in all periods and genres of English and Scottish Literature, including Literary Theory (especially Gender). For further information please contact Dr. Ian Johnson, Director of Postgraduate Studies, on (01334) 462666.

◆ School Geography and Geology (Division of Human Geography)

The School houses three active research groups in the following areas of **Human Geography**: Urban and Regional Studies, Development and Population Studies, Historical and Cultural Geography. Both 3-year Ph.D. and 2-year M.Phil. research degrees are offered and interdisciplinary as well as policy-oriented research is encouraged. Postgraduate funding (at ESRC rates) is available for research in a relevant aspect of **contemporary China**. For further information contact Professor Chris Smith (e-mail: cjs15@st-and.ac.uk). See Web Page http://www.st-and.ac.uk/~www_sgg/ggdept.htm1.

◆ School of Mathematical and Computational Sciences

There are research groups in algebra, analysis, approximation theory and numerical analysis, fluid mechanics and nonlinear evolution equations, solar theory, theoretical plasma physics, statistics, algebraic and logical computation, algorithms, parallel and distributed computation, and persistent programming systems. Programmes of study are available for Ph.D. and M.Sc. degrees. E-mail enquiries may be sent to research.enquiries@dcs.st-and.ac.uk. Our WWW page is at http://www.dcs.st-and.ac.uk/Rsch/.

◆ School of Psychology

The School comprises one of the best and most comprehensively equipped psychological laboratories in the UK and has a thriving research community as evidenced by the maximum rating for research in all of the Research Assessment Exercises. The School particularly welcomes Ph.D. and M.Phil. applications in the following areas: Cognition and Perception, Computational and Behavioural Neuroscience, Evolutionary Studies, Heath Psychology, Neuropsychology, and Social and Forensic Psychology. Enquiries and applications to the Convener, Postgraduate Committee, School of Psychology, University of St Andrews, Fife, KY16 9JU.

THE UNIVERSITY *of* LIVERPOOL

Postgraduate Study at the University of Liverpool

The University of Liverpool is proud of its international reputation for quality research with excellent facilities and a lively, dynamic atmosphere in which to study.

The University's four **Graduate Schools** foster research across traditional departmental boundaries, and act as a focus for postgraduate activity. Research leading to the degrees of **MPhil** and **PhD** are available across all the disciplines represented by the Graduate Schools, which are:

Biological and Biomedical Sciences

Economic and Social Sciences (including Law)

Engineering and Physical Sciences

Humanities

In addition, **taught courses** leading to Postgraduate Diplomas and Masters degrees are offered in the following general subject areas:

Humanities	**Social Sciences**	**Environmental Studies**
Languages	**Law**	**Life Sciences**
Earth Sciences	**Physical Sciences**	**Engineering**
Medicine/Health Sciences	**Veterinary Science**	**Business & Management**

For more information
Why not visit the University's Homepage at **http://www.liv.ac.uk**? Individual
Graduate School pages are also under construction – visit Humanities at
http://www.liv.ac.uk/-hgs/

or contact:
Postgraduate Admissions Service, The University of Liverpool, Schools, Colleges,
International Liaison and Admissions Service (SCILAS), Student Services Centre,
150 Mount Pleasant, Liverpool L69 3GD, UK.
Tel: 44(0)151 794 2069   Fax: 44(0)151 794 2060   Email: scilas@liverpool.ac.uk

For the Advancement of Learning

CONTENTS

1 INTRODUCTION

The number of students opting for postgraduate study is increasing all the time. Over 315,000 now do so (compared with 100,000 12 years ago). This figure represents 20% of the total higher education student population. Why do they do it? After all, further years of study represent these days a considerable financial investment – not to mention loss of possible earnings and a step on the promotion ladder.

It seems unlikely that the majority of these students have suddenly been seized by a thirst for further knowledge. Some will have been of course, and would want to develop an academic interest come what may. Others, though, may have been affected by a lack of suitable graduate employment opportunities. Although percentage-wise graduates still enjoy the lowest unemployment rate, they do not all find jobs in the area of their first choice. Some then are taking further courses in an effort to impress employers and steal an edge in the market. The explosion in the numbers of undergraduates being admitted to degree courses – up 17% in ten years – has brought a consequent increase in the supply of graduates available. We may be heading for the situation common in some countries, where to gain a job which once would have been done by a graduate it is necessary to have a master's or similar level of qualification. Others may find that although a considerable number of graduate vacancies (35%) are still advertised as being open to graduates in any discipline, a conversion course in a vocational area may enhance their prospects. Then, some jobs have always required master's level qualifications. Yet other careers have a relevant postgraduate degree or diploma as the minimum entry requirement. The qualification is actually the licence to practise a profession, as in teaching or social work.

The greatest boom has been in the area of taught master's courses – and this had led to some disquiet regarding uniformity of standards.

The question of quality has been addressed recently in the Harris Report. The committee, chaired by Professor Harris of Manchester University, recommended a code of practice to the Committee of Vice Chancellors and Principals regarding minimum standards to be adhered to in establishing new courses. It also made its findings known to the funding councils which give financial support to courses. (The question of quality is dealt with in more detail in Chapter 8.)

Why then should you consider postgraduate study? Assuming that you have made the decision, how do you set about finding the right course? And, most important, how will you finance it? This book attempts to answer or give you some pointers to answering these and other questions.

With thanks to the people who agreed to be interviewed for this book and to Jamie Darwen, Chair of the National Postgraduate Committee for his assistance.

2 WHY TAKE A POSTGRADUATE COURSE ?

The number of postgraduates is increasing. But taking a postgraduate course is a major decision: – one year's sacrificed earnings at the very least. (Unless your reason for considering postgraduate study at all is that you haven't been able to find a job.) Add to that the fact that the year may be going to cost you something in the region of several thousand pounds – and you have to be sure that the investment will be worth it. Is postgraduate study always a good idea?

As with any other decision, there are potential advantages and possible drawbacks.

THE PROS AND CONS

The reasons for people choosing to take postgraduate courses have been touched on in the introduction. Each has its plus points – but there are also some, not always immediately obvious, drawbacks. You should weigh everything up very carefully.

I enjoy my degree subject and I want to go into some aspect of it in further depth. Surely that is a good enough reason?

It is an excellent reason. You will be highly motivated and interested. You will prove to yourself that you are capable of further in-depth study and there are lots of opportunities to specialise. There are languages graduates taking higher courses in linguistics or interpreting, engineers studying robotics, mathematicians doing actuarial studies, historians specialising in the period of Richard ll, geographers studying environmental processes or demography . . . and so on. But

where do you expect it to lead? Have you thought about a possible career? So long as you are not banking on an academic career . . . There are not enough university lectureships to go round.

I wish I'd done a different subject. The one I touched on as a minor subject interested me far more than my major. If I can find a department that will accept me, I'd like to change direction.

Fine – but see above.

Won't an extra year give me more time to find out what I want to do in life?

Not really. Not unless you use some of the time to investigate career possibilities and spend some time in the careers advisory service reading room. A career inspiration won't suddenly drop in on you out of the blue. But yes, if you really are uncertain, a postgraduate year can buy you extra time.

Will a postgraduate course give me stronger qualifications?

Yes, and for many research-based careers further qualifications are almost mandatory.

Will it get me a better job?

This is one of the common – but potentially dangerous reasons given for choosing postgraduate study. Not all employers value postgraduate work. There are many who would prefer to have you a year earlier and start to train you in their methods.

I have a humanities degree, so surely I should take a year to do a course in something more relevant to a career, like business studies?

Again, not necessarily. In some fields it helps to add a more specific second qualification to a first degree. In others not so much. Commerce for instance, is one of those areas which contains many employers who are happy to take finalists from all kinds of degree disciplines. There are classics graduates working in merchant banks, historians in retail management, English graduates in insurance companies.

Val Butcher, who is the Assistant Director of Leeds University's careers advisory service, is often consulted by undergraduates wondering whether or not to take a postgraduate course. She says, 'They really must do so in the context of life planning. They need to ask themselves why they want to do the course; whether the course is for their personal satisfaction or whether it is necessary. If it is a vocational course, is it absolutely essential like a course in librarianship, or would it be helpful as opposed to essential, in a competitive area? The media is one example where a course can help, although this is not always so much from the course content as from contacts students are able to make.'

'Unfortunately, some institutions have rushed to establish postgraduate courses that do not necessarily enhance students' marketability. Given the cost of taking a course, students must check out things like job prospects, employment rates, practical experience provided and the course organiser's contacts in a given industry.'

Roger Brown is also a careers adviser. He says, 'Some master's courses are useful to top up a first degree, and give a vocational bias to the student's studies. But courses perceived as vocational do not always greatly enhance employment options. There are many postgraduate courses in economics, banking and finance, but they are not always that attractive to employers. In contrast, it's more normal to top up a computer science degree with a more specialised MSc in, for instance, systems engineering and artificial intelligence.'

Students often ask Roger about employers' attitudes to a master's course. 'That's a difficult one. It's certainly better than being unemployed or taking a very low level job, but it should not be seen as a magic formula. Personal qualities, motivation and the whole personal package count when job hunting. These aren't necessarily improved on during a master's year. Relevant vacation work, placements on courses and work experience are important when trying to impress an employer.' But see below.*

Will I need a postgraduate qualification to enter the career of my choice?

In many cases, yes. You must have a Postgraduate Certificate in Education (PGCE), for example, if you wish to teach in a state school (but not always to work in the private sector). You would need a diploma in social work in order to work as a social worker (but this can be obtained in employment), a master's degree in information management/science or diploma in librarianship to work in librarianship and sometimes in information management jobs, a master's or doctorate to become a clinical psychologist and a law diploma in order to practise as a solicitor or barrister. These types of course are covered more fully in Chapter 5.

I've been told that in many cases I'll stand a better chance of getting into the career I want if I take a master's course. Is this true? *

Yes, even though there are some career areas and specific employers who are happy to recruit graduates from any discipline, there are a large number who give preference to graduates who have topped up their first degree with a relevant diploma. Examples include personnel management, leisure and tourism management, and journalism. In addition, there are some degrees which although relevant to a career have not, with some exceptions, taught all the skills required to earn a living in one particular field. An example that springs immediately to mind is that of languages degrees. Most graduates hoping to work as translators or interpreters feel the need for a further course – although this is not essential, and some do set up, particularly as freelance translators, without doing so. Journalism, publishing and the media in general are areas where competition is so intense that possession of a relevant postgraduate qualification can put graduates at an advantage. Roger Brown finds that there is a lot

of interest in the media but says students must be cautious about postgraduate options. He does recommend courses like the journalism courses at City University, Cardiff and the London College of Printing, whilst other courses are difficult to assess. (There is a caveat however: 'But students must be the right sort of people, preferably with relevant work experience on student or local newspapers'.)

Would it give me more opportunity to work abroad?

There are certainly some countries, particularly the USA and some European Union countries, where a master's qualification makes students much more attractive to employers.

I seem to have taken completely the wrong degree subject. Now what can I do?

Take a postgraduate conversion course. You could for instance take a course in planning if your first degree does not have sufficient relevant content, or a law diploma (Common Professional Examination or CPE) if you are a non-law graduate. Some students with first degrees in human sciences follow these with a master's degree or diploma in psychology in order to become eligible for professional training.

TRANSFERABLE SKILLS

It would be wise to bear in mind all the above warnings with regard to checking validity of qualifications in the employment market. Yes, employers may not always regard postgraduate qualifications as necessary. Yes, they may question the value of a further academic course. BUT those who recruit graduates of any discipline always say that they are looking for personal skills rather than subject-specific knowledge. On many courses you should acquire transferable skills, a common requirement in most jobs.

What are these?

- Self sufficiency.
- Time management. Postgraduate courses are intensive. To accomplish everything in the time required demands the abilities to concentrate, to work hard and to prioritise.
- Communication skills – from presenting papers and reasoned arguments.
- The ability to locate information fast and accurately – and to use it for a specific purpose.
- And, depending on the course, the ability to work with others in a team. Many employers prize this skill. It is inbuilt in many courses that emphasise project work.

Research students in science subjects who are placed in teams may not always realise that they are acquiring this ability, but they are working with, co-operating with and negotiating with other people constantly.

CHECKLIST OF QUESTIONS TO ASK

- Why do I *really* want to do further study?
- Why this course?
- What will it give me?
- Where will it take me?
- Is my interest strong enough to study one aspect in depth? (Academic courses)
- Is it worth the year's loss of income through not starting work?
- Can I afford it?

TO SUM UP

If you are considering taking a vocational course of any kind, it is a good idea to use your careers service to check out the value of the proposed qualification and also to check with prospective employers.

Where an academic course is concerned the same sources should be consulted. You will want also to ask advice from academic departments – your present one and the ones where you are considering studying.

3 ENTRY REQUIREMENTS

WHAT CLASS OF FIRST DEGREE WILL I NEED IN ORDER TO UNDERTAKE FURTHER STUDY?

That depends partly on the level of the course and partly on your funding requirements!

In general, the minimum stipulated requirement for a **higher degree course** is a 'good honours degree'. This can mean a lower second. In practice, it usually means an upper second – although criteria can vary with different admissions tutors and, let's be honest, the popularity of the course in question.

IF your heart is set on doing a certain course and you do not achieve a first or upper second, all is not lost. It could be worth doing a master's (always assuming that you can get a place for that!). A lower second plus a master's *may* equate to an upper second.

The entry requirements to **diploma** and **certificate** courses are less rigid because very often some relevant work experience and/or personal qualities are taken into account. But some courses do have a minimum requirement. The CPE law course, for example, stipulates an upper second.

Why should funding make a difference?

Because there are not sufficient funds to pay for every place available on courses. The Funding Councils, which are the main providers of awards to postgraduate students, can ask for high standards. Competition for their awards is severe. Many of the awards given by the British Academy (the major funder of arts and humanities courses), for example, are given to students with firsts. The Academy's handbook states, 'The number of applicants with first class degrees, and in the competition for three year awards, with highly graded postgraduate experience, substantially exceeds the total number of awards available.' The Medical Research Council had 236 applications for 55 advanced course studentships last year.

It is perfectly possible – unfortunately all too common – to gain a place on a course but be refused any kind of grant. More of this later in Chapter 11.

SPECIAL ENTRANCE TESTS

For some courses you would be expected to take an additional entry test.

International students coming to the UK might, for instance, have to take one of the recognised tests in English: students applying for MBAs, the GMAT test. (More on these in the relevant chapters.)

ALTERNATIVE QUALIFICATIONS

There are alternative qualifications which may help you to gain acceptance on to a course – and they don't always have to be pieces of paper. Under a scheme known as APEL, Accreditation of Prior Experiental Learning, you could be given credit for either previous qualifications, such as those awarded by professional bodies or for relevant experience at an appropriate level in employment. Requests for APEL have to be accompanied by supporting evidence – either proof of qualifications or full testimonials from employers.

APEL could ease acceptance on to a course. It can also exempt you from taking part of it. Admittedly, it is normally more applicable to vocational than to academic courses.

HOW DO I KNOW THAT I AM SUITABLE FOR HIGHER LEVEL WORK?

Some honest self-assessment comes in here. Have you had to work at full stretch in order to graduate this year? Found it a bit of a grind? Secretly felt that other students are much more gifted than you? OR have you sailed through your degree course? Wondered where the time has gone? Longed to spend more time on one aspect of the syllabus?

Other people's assessment counts too. Without a good academic reference an application form for an advanced course doesn't get a look in.

PERSONAL QUALITIES

Postgraduate work is hard and very different from undergraduate work. Are you a good time manager?

If you are considering research in the humanities, much of your work will be done on your own. Although your superviser should be a source of support, for much of the time you will be dependent on your own resources. Do you **enjoy** working alone? Have you got the necessary self discipline?

One way of finding out whether you might enjoy doctoral research is to take a master's first and find out something of what the work for a doctoral thesis would involve.

Leiden University
Faculty of Law

Leiden is a historic city and a genuine university town situated near the political and economical heart of the Netherlands. It lies 17 km northeast of The Hague, the Dutch political and administrative centre and the legal centre of the world (International Court of Justice, International Criminal Tribunal for the former Yugoslavia, tran-US Claims Tribunal), and 41 km southwest of Amsterdam. For more than four centuries Leiden University has been a respected, internationally oriented University of the highest standing. The Faculty of Law is conscious of the increasing need for all lawyers increasingly will require to be trained to confront problems which transcend national frontiers.

Master of Laws
The Faculty of Law offers highly motivated law graduates three intensive one-year, full-time postgraduate programmes leading to the degree of Master of Laws (LL.M).

LL.M. in Public International Law: Core courses include: Public International Law, International Peacekeeping, Accountability of International Organisations, External Relations of the European Union. Sustainable Development, Protection of Human Rights, Humanitarian Law of Armed Conflict, State Creation & Self Determination.

LL.M. in European Community Law: After an introductory semester (EC-Law and Private International Law) the emphasis is placed on the substantive law of the EC (Competition Law, Corporate Law, Tax Law, Intellectual Property Law, Business Law, Human Rights Law and the Law of the External Relations of th EC).

LL.M. in Criminology: After an introduction to general criminological subjects the participants are offered the possibility of getting acquainted with the specialists of Dutch Criminology and Criminal Policies by lectures, participation in practical work at different Dutch Institutions and joining research done in the Criminology Institute. The LL.M. in Criminology is open to only a few students every year.

Assessment of the three programmes is by examination, essays and a dissertation. The programmes start in September. All lecturers and seminars are in English.
An applicant to the LL.M. Programme must satisfy two basic requirements: 1) completion of a degree in law, and 2) proficiency in written and spoken English. For the LL.M in Criminology also a special science degree is accepted.

For further information contact:
Leiden Law Programmes, Office of Administrations, Faculty of Law,
University of Leiden, P.O. Box 9521, 2300 RA Leiden, The Netherlands.
Tel: (+31) 71 527 7672; Fax: (+31) 71 527 7732:
E-mail: jfhioms@Ruljur.LeidenUniv.NL

4 DIFFERENT LEVELS OF COURSE AND METHODS OF STUDY

There are more than 5,000 postgraduate courses on offer. All universities and a number of colleges and institutes of higher education run programmes of some kind beyond first degree level – although not every subject or course is offered everywhere.

There are also different modes of study. Some qualifications are achieved on taught courses, some by research only and others by a combination of the two methods.

Postgraduate courses come with all sorts of names. The generic titles are:

- Master's degrees:- MA or MSc are the most usual, but just as there are first degrees with different titles, some master's degrees are, for example, MMus, MEd or LLM (law). A well known one is the MBA. Then there is the MPhil, a research degree.
- Doctorates
- Diplomas or certificates.

HOW DO I KNOW WHICH SORT OF COURSE WOULD BE RIGHT?

The terms used to describe most postgraduate courses are fairly familiar, but you may not know just which one is the one you should be aiming at. Basically, you choose between a higher degree, diploma or certificate and between a taught or research programme.

WHAT IS A HIGHER DEGREE?

There are two kinds: master's degrees and doctorates.

Master's degrees

The majority of postgraduate courses fall into this category and it is the fastest expanding area. An MSc or MA is awarded according to the area of study. MScs cover science, engineering and technical subjects, but are also sometimes awarded in business studies and the social sciences such as economics. MAs are for the arts and humanities – but there are exceptions with some business and social science courses leading to an MA. As always, it is not the title of the course so much as its content that is relevant.

Master's degrees may be followed on a taught programme or research basis.

Master's courses *used* to last for one year and the majority were taught. (See Chapter 7.) However, increasing numbers of two year programmes are being established, as are master's degrees by research (usually Master of Philosophy or MPhil). MPhil degrees are at a higher level than MAs and MScs but below that of a doctorate. (They can be awarded for arts, social studies or science degrees.)

Doctorates

PhDs (Doctor of Philosophy) are always achieved by research under the guidance of a supervisor – a member of academic staff who shares the student's interest and is expert in that particular area. The student must also submit a thesis – of up to 100,000 words – which shows evidence of original scholarship and can be prepared for publication. The title Doctor of Philosophy, usually PhD or sometimes DPhil, is awarded in all disciplines – arts and sciences alike.

A degree obtained through research consists of highly specialised study, is largely self-directed and the research must be original. A PhD typically takes three years (but can take longer) and culminates in the writing of a thesis. An MPhil normally takes two years.

There are now some taught doctorate programmes which are different from PhDs in that they are confined to vocational areas such as education, business studies or engineering.

WHAT IS THE DIFFERENCE BETWEEN DEGREE AND CERTIFICATE OR DIPLOMA COURSES?

Certificates and diplomas are nearly always vocational. Some lead to a specific qualification required to practise a profession, for example the PGCE (teaching); some are linked to a particular group of careers, for example the media. Most of the conversion courses available also come into this category. Because they have a specific purpose, they are more structured than the postgraduate degree courses and concentrate on preparing students for the related career.

It is sometimes possible to convert a diploma or certificate into a Master's degree by completing a project or writing a dissertation.

METHODS OF STUDY

Almost equal numbers of students are now studying for higher qualifications full time and part time.

Full time

This is obviously the fastest route to a qualification, but does depend on your having sufficient financial resources. (Some of the awards and bursaries available are only given to full time students.)

It is still more common at the moment to start postgraduate study in the natural sciences straight from a first degree course and to do them full time.

Are courses always full time?

No. More and more people want to combine study with earning, or alternatively with bringing up a family. The most difficult to do on a part time basis while in employment are the taught master's courses, because of their intensive nature and emphasis on practical work and experience. But it can be done – by finding a university or college that allows students to complete them over a longer period and puts on longer courses, say two years.

Taught higher degrees can often be done part-time over a longer period and many people complete research degrees by part time study – over five to six years, often while in full time work.

Part time study is on the increase because of the difficulty of finding funding for the full time route.

Part time – is part time study a realistic option?

Yes, very much so. There have been no cuts or blocks on providing postgraduate programmes as there have been on undergraduate level work. Postgraduate students are an important source of income to higher education institutions. Universities and the colleges of higher education which undertake postgraduate work are in competition for postgraduates, who are fast entering a buyers' market. Courses are being set up all the time with the needs of the consumer in mind.

If the course you would like to take does not seem to be available by part time study or distance learning today – it might be tomorrow. In the meantime it is always worth enquiring and negotiating.

The number of part time postgraduate students is on the up, and is for several reasons. One is of simple economics. Financing part time study while in employment is an attractive option for many students. Postgraduates have always had to prepare to finance themselves, but now that so many graduate from first degree courses in debt, many are becoming reluctant to take out further loans. Another is that if the qualification is vocationally relevant, some assistance may be available from employers. In some career areas, notably management and technology, employers often encourage their staff to work for higher degrees and offer assistance for them to do so, either in the form of payment of fees or of time off to attend courses, sometimes both. Some employers are particularly keen to assist employees to obtain MBAs. Others sponsor MScs and PhDs.

As a result, postgraduate courses have become more flexible. Some are organised into intensive periods of teaching. Students attend in the evening or over weekends – perhaps for a week long course with their employer's permission. Projects and dissertations may be linked to the workplace, giving the employer the benefit of research directly linked to improving some aspect of their business, and the student the opportunity to conduct further study after relevant experience – which can make the research both more interesting and more relevant.

Distance Learning

Studying may not involve much attendance at formal courses or even any at all. There are already master's degrees based on electronic mail, and the Open University runs a 'virtual' summer school through the same means. The Open University, of course, has always worked on this method and meets the needs of many postgraduates. Other universities have now joined in – and there are even facilities, through CATS, to gain credit for work done at some different universities, and between them and the Open University.

How does it work?

You would be provided with course material and reading lists and would be set assignments to be handed in and marked by a tutor. Distance learning these days is light years away from the old correspondence courses and is a popular method of study in all kinds of areas. Study is supplemented by meetings between students and tutors. Sometimes, local study and support groups are established. Weekend courses and summer schools may also be available.

Can every course be followed by this method?

It is more difficult, though not impossible, for scientists and engineers who need access to laboratories. If they are in relevant employment and can use employers' facilities it becomes more feasible.

What is CATS?

The Credit Accumulation and Transfer System. It is a system under which people can gain credit for a module of study. When sufficient credits – which are all given a CATS rating – have been collected, a particular qualification can be claimed. A first degree for instance takes 360 points, a taught master's 120 'M' level ones.

You cannot simply choose modules and pick up credits for them as though shopping in a supermarket though. The modules must be relevant to a programme of study and negotiation has to take place. You would have to persuade one institution to accept some of the credits in your shopping basket when applying to register for a course. Many advanced short courses are now being given credit ratings and it has become possible to use some of these towards a postgraduate degree at some universities. This can be particularly useful for someone who decides to enrol for a postgraduate qualification after some years at work – and finds that they already have some credit towards part of it.

CATS is also useful to people who are moving around the country in the course of their employment, which is quite common for graduates in the early stages of a career. It makes part time study over several years quite feasible.

The Open University

The Open University offers the following postgraduate programmes:

- MA in Humanities
- MA in Education

- MA in Open and Distance Education
- MSc in Mathematics
- MSc in Computing for Commerce and Industry
- MSc in Manufacturing, Management and Technology
- The MBA
- The MBA (Technology Management)
- PGCE
- Doctorate in Education (EdD)
- Research degrees.

Taught Courses

All the higher degree programmes require students to complete 180 OU points of appropriate courses – which would be the equivalent of one and a half years' full time study and equate to 120 M level CATS points.

The entry requirement is normally an upper second.

Programmes in Education

- The 18 month PGCE includes 18 weeks of school experience.
- The EdD programme is acquired through a combination of taught courses and research leading to a dissertaion.

Research programmes

Research programmes lead to the awards of BPhil, MPhil or PhD. Students arrange to meet their supervisors at mutually convenient times. If necessary, they may be given assistance in obtaining access to suitable libraries in their home areas. Not all research students are part time however. The University has 220 students studying full time. They work either at the University's headquarters in Milton Keynes, at its Research Unit in Oxford or, for certain projects, at one of the University's 13 Regional Centres. Facilities – libraries, laboratories and personal computers are provided, as are individual work places in shared offices.

The entry requirement is normally an upper second.

FACTS AND FIGURES

- Approximately equal numbers of students opt for full time research and taught degree courses – around 44,500 for each.
- Among part time higher degree students, 72,100 – two thirds – are on taught courses, mainly Masters.
- 49% of full time postgraduates are 25 years or over.
- 90% of part time postgraduates are 25 years or over.

Total numbers of students (full and part time)

Doctorates by research	58,100
Taught Doctorates	400
Masters by research	30,900
Taught Masters	120,200
Other higher degrees	7,000

Other postgraduate courses:

Diplomas or certificates	58,800
Professional qualifications	6,500
Diplomas or certificates plus professional qualifications	7,100
Degree plus professional qualification	9,000
PGCE	21,500

5 TYPES OF COURSE

The different levels of qualification were described in Chapter 4. Here we look at types of course.

A. ESSENTIAL

In some situations it is essential to study for a postgraduate qualification in order to practise a particular profession. There are also some postgraduate courses which are necessary if an initial vocational course in the chosen area has not been taken – as for example, in teaching. Some examples are as follows:

- Art therapy
- Careers guidance
- Clinical psychology
- Conservation of textiles and works of art
- Dance therapy
- Drama therapy
- Educational psychology
- Educational welfare work
- Health promotion and education
- Law – barrister: non-law graduates must take a CPE followed by the vocational course at the Inns of Court Law School.
- Law – solicitor: non-law graduates must take a CPE course, followed by the LPC course – both one year.
  (Students who are certain they intend to become solicitors may take the Diploma in Law as an alternative to the CPE).
- Librarianship
- Music therapy
- Occupational therapy
- Overseas development work
- Psychotherapy
- Research and development

- Social work
- Speech therapy
- Youth and community work
- Teaching.

Some examples follow of courses which are essential if you want to enter particular professions.

Diploma in Social Work (recognised by the Central Council for Education and Training in Social Work)

Full time, two years.

The programme 'aims to train reflective practitioners who work in an anti-oppressive way and are able to help people appropriately.' It consists of two periods of time at the university plus placements and a final period at the university.

Year 1 studies include: situations encountered in practice, frames of reference, social policy, interviewing skills, research, law, ethics and values, race and anti-racist practice plus user involvement.

Year 2 studies include: pursuit of particular areas of practice and work with a range of client groups.

Assessment is by evaluation of written work and a report prepared by practice teachers.

Common Professional Examination

(for non-law graduates)

One year full time or two years part time.

The course 'provides a speedy route for non-law graduates to progress to the Solicitors' or Barristers' Finals course'.

The part time routes can be either two days per week or mixed day and evening attendance. The full time course consists of seven core subjects: tort, contract, constitutional and administrative law, equity and trusts, land law, criminal law and European law. Part time students attend the same classes as full time students but take three subjects per year.

The course commences with a two week induction programme which includes workshops on techniques and requirements for the study of law, use of law library, court visit and lectures. The main programme is taught by a variety of lectures and tutorials. Students usually also participate in other activities, including moots, visits and guest lectures.

Assessment is by final examination (75%) and by an assessed coursework assignment in each subject (25%).

Postgraduate Diploma in Art Therapy

Two year full time or three to four part time.

In Year 1 the emphasis is on the taught aspects of the training and on supervised placements.

Year 2 places more emphasis on clinical placement work, writing of case studies and a dissertation.

The structure is: two days per week in college during year 1 and one day per week in college during year 2 plus two days per week in clinical placements. The rest of the week is allocated for independent study and in Year 2 there are special subject seminars. The course is supported by individual tutorials.

The course includes: nature and process of art, fieldwork, thematic workshops, personal creativity, art therapy studies, psychotherapy, experiential workshops, psychiatry, therapy skills, psychology and case presentation skills.

Assessment takes the form of: written assignments; exams including psychiatry, psychology, psychotherapy; evaluation of placement work and a 5,000 word dissertation.

Postgraduate Certificate in Education (Primary)

Full time, one year (38 weeks over three academic terms).

The work of the course in college is closely related to work with children in school.

Students spend time in school:

Term 1, one day per week plus three separate weeks (in week five, nine and ten of the term);

Term 2, the first three and a half weeks then one day per week for the rest of the term;

Term 3, the first eight and a half weeks.

Through a mixture of lectures and seminars, students study child development, children's learning, school and classroom management, plus the content and process of learning and teaching of particular curriculum i.e. English, mathematics, science, design and technology, geography, history, music, art, physical education and religious education.

Students are expected to spend the first two weeks of the course in school, for which they make their own arrangements.

Assessment is based upon practical teaching and three major assignments. There are no examinations.

Ann Henderson is a careers adviser at King Alfred's College in Winchester. She has some particular advice for students contemplating a

PGCE. 'Please make sure that you want to teach. It is easy to fall into the trap of wanting to concentrate on a favourite subject (history for example) and to think of teaching as a conduit for this. This may not necessarily be the case. A teacher's role is to teach – the subject is secondary. So please think very carefully about this as the PGCE year is a busy one, full of hard work. You do not want to waste a year of your time.

'This applies particularly to primary school teaching where, as a teacher, you do not concentrate on one subject. You may be responsible for its development through the school, but your pupils expect you to teach them most, if not all, subjects.

'If you are in any doubt as to whether teaching is the right route for you, arrange some visits to schools. A range of schools is advisable so that you build up a broad picture, and this also gives you the chance to seek advice and guidance from a wide range of teachers – for example: urban, rural, private, state, primary, secondary, junior, middle, college, small, large, church maintained, single sex, mixed, grammar, secondary, comprehensive or tertiary.'

B. CONVERSION COURSES

These are designed, as the name implies, to enable graduates from one discipline to study another. They are normally vocational courses, to train students with non-relevant degrees for a particular career.

One example is the one year course in information technology which exists at more than 50 institutions. Graduates from any discipline are accepted – and train for careers in computing departments and software companies.

Other examples include:

- Biomedical engineering (from biology)
- Engineering (from a science degree)

- International business or marketing (usually from a degree in languages)
- Law (any discipline)
- Pharmacology (related science degree)
- Secretarial/secretarial linguist (any discipline or languages degree respectively).

For example:

Postgraduate Diploma in Information Technology

Full time, one year.

There are two parallel intakes. The Applied Information Systems stream is a general conversion course open to anyone who meets the entry requirements. The Business Information Systems stream is specifically designed for female applicants in response to EU recommendations (satisfies Section 47 of the Sex Discrimination Act).

The courses are geared to the needs of today's high-tech world and emphasise practical IT applications coupled with relevant technical skills. They include: database management systems, introduction to information technology, information systems environment, application software development, systems analysis and design plus business computing systems. Students also address data protection and legal topics as well as undergoing assertiveness training. Presentation and interpersonal skills are also developed culminating in a final project, on which a written report and presentation must be given.

Course subjects are assessed on a continuous basis.

C. 'DESIRABLE'

There are many careers for which a postgraduate course is useful but not essential. These are also conversion courses of a kind, but are usually aimed at very specific careers.

Courses which may be of great benefit if you hope to enter a chosen career

- Archaeology
- Archive studies and conservation
- Art gallery studies
- Arts administration
- Cartography
- Economic forecasting
- Forensic science
- Heritage management
- Hotel and hospitality management
- Housing management
- Journalism
- Leisure and recreation management
- Management studies
- Museum studies
- Occupational hygiene
- Personnel work
- Publishing
- Tourism.

It is always important to check the situation for each specific profession. Careers adviser Ann Henderson says, 'In some cases a postgraduate qualification is essential; in others it is helpful. You will, no doubt, already have some idea of this. Check all your facts – and double check them. This is important as one piece of literature may be misleading. It is always useful to check with the professional body, institute or advisory body for the career in which you are interested.'

For example:

Postgraduate Diploma in Journalism

Full time, nine month course.

Students specialise in newspaper, magazine, broadcast journalism or media relations.

The objective is to 'teach the craft of journalism against a background of professional studies'. All students must be able to type fluently before the start of the course.

Compulsory background studies include media law, public administration and the relationship between journalism and society. The course includes regular production days when students find and write news and features, exactly as they would for newspapers, magazines and broadcasting stations. Media relations students work on actual projects for outside public bodies, charities and commercial organisations.

Work attachments are arranged during the Easter vacation at leading newspapers, magazines, radio/TV stations. Media relations students join the press offices of various organisations. Facilities include a computer editorial system and a computerised broadcast newsroom.

Assessment: 60% by continuous assessment of practical work – which includes a major research project in the final term; 40% by final examinations. Background studies are assessed by combination of term papers and final examinations.

MA in Gallery Studies

Full time, one year.

'A practical and theoretical training for those concerned with devising or curating exhibitions.' Students choose two sections or specialisations in the form of a two hour seminar over 20 weeks. One of these may be outside the specialist MA course. Methods of teaching include weekly seminars, practical workshops, on-site visits and interviews. Facilities include the University's own gallery which acts as the local point for the promotion of the visual arts on campus. Students from the MA Gallery studies course organise one or more of the six major exhibitions scheduled each year. Student participation is encouraged at every stage on the implementation of the programme.

Assessment is by four major essays and either a 20,000 word dissertation or an exhibition.

MSc in Business and Management

Full time for 12 months.

The course 'gives students a thorough introduction to essential management concepts, tools, functions and disciplines as well as an understanding of business policy and planning.' Subjects studied include: business and management, business economics, quantitative methods, computing and information systems, managerial accounting, human resource management, marketing management, operations management, finance and financial management, business policy and business planning and research methodology. Workshops are run on business simulation and personal and managerial skills. Students are taught by a variety of methods including lectures, case studies, workshops, use of video observation and market research (on the street!).

Assessment is by continuous assessment and final examinations. Students must also pursue three electives and submit a final project.

Postgraduate Diploma in Hotel Catering and Management

Full time, one year.

The course is accredited by the Hotel Catering and Institutional Management Association. 'This is an expressly vocational course providing an intensive series of studies to develop knowledge and skills in relevant business and technical subjects.' Prior to enrolment all students are expected to have undertaken at least six weeks employment in the industry. Units studied include: foundation studies, management skills workshop, managing people, managing environmental influences (hospitality marketing and business economics), managing finance, and managing operations (accommodation management, food and beverage management, facilities management, strategic management). Students also undertake an integrative project. Emphasis is placed throughout upon the development of a realistic appreciation of the operating standards appropriate to the provision of customer satisfaction in a service industry.

Assessment combines continuous coursework monitoring and formal examinations.

MA in Applied Translation Studies

One year, full time.

The course consists of lectures, seminars and practical classes for two eleven week semesters. The summer is devoted to writing a dissertation or preparing two extended translations. Students select a range of modules from a list which includes: research methods, translating general/literary, technical writing, translators' tools, informatics and translation, machine assisted translation (MAT), expert systems, advanced translation, variety and accents of English, consecutive bilateral interpreting, socio-linguistics, text processing by computer, area studies and British studies. Native English speakers normally offer two of the languages from the list available. An optional module in consecutive bilateral interpreting is also available.

Assessment is a mix of continuous assessment and closed examinations. In addition, students present either a 10,000 word dissertation on a topic in the field of translation studies or submit two 4,000–5,000 word extended translations with an accompanying linguistic and stylistic commentary. (For students with two languages, it would be expected that translations would be from each of the languages).

MA in Mediterranean Archaeology

Course content: compulsory skills courses in research methods, use of sources such as the National Monuments Record, the National

Birkbeck College UNIVERSITY OF LONDON

Department of Economics

MSc Economics

Two years part-time; one year full-time, this course is designed to develop a critical understanding of economic theories and their application to current economic problems. The department is especially strong in macroeconomics policy and applied econometrics.

MSc Finance

Two years part-time; one year full-time, this course offers specialised training in financial econometrics and international finance and should appeal to those interested in policy questions associated with financial markets.

Postgraduate Certificate in Economics or Finance

These are programmes in their own right or act as conversion courses for those who wish to continue to the MSc in Economics or Finance. One year part-time.

For further details contact: Postgraduate Admissions Secretary, Department of Economics, 7-15 Gresse Street, London W1P 2LL. Tel: 0171 631 6429 or Email: courses@econ.bbk.ac.uk http://www.econ.bbk.ac.uk

Department of Management and Business Studies

MSc International Business

Two years part-time; one year full-time commencing 1997/98, this degree programme aims to equip students with the tools and techniques to learn to operate effectively in an international business situation.

Postgraduate Certificate in Accountancy and Management

One year part-time, this is an accredited course by the Institute of Chartered Accountants in England and Wales. It is a conversion course suitable for graduates who would like to enter the accountancy profession or to familiarise themselves with basic accounting, and business concepts and techniques.

part-time & full-time study opportunities

BIRKBECK COLLEGE
UNIVERSITY OF LONDON

For further details contact: The Department Secretary, Graduate Admissions, Department of Management and Business Studies, Birkbeck College, University of London, 7-15 Gresse Street, London W1P 2LL Tel: 0171 631 6767 or Email: p.tolentino@mbs.bbk.ac.uk

Archaeological Record and County Sites and Monuments Records, maps and bibliography, computing, plus tuition in surveying, excavation techniques, and a foreign language; either a broad view of the development of historic and prehistoric societies around the Mediterranean basin or specialism in either historic or prehistoric archaeology, and optional courses including, the Emergence of Civilisation in the Aegean, the Archaeology of Cyprus, Prehistoric Societies in the Mediterranean, the Roman Mediterranean, The City of Rome, Art and Society.

Assessed by essays and a 20,000 word dissertation.

D. ACADEMIC COURSES

These are the courses in which you would study a subject or a specialist topic in depth. They enable you to delve deeper into an area of your undergraduate degree that you particularly enjoyed but were not able to devote sufficient time to.

Examples of courses include:

MA in German

Course content: two major options, for example Literary Theory and Method, Modes of Narrative from Romanticism to the Present, and two minor options, for example Women's Writing in German, Poetics and Experiment: words and image.

Assessed by four termly papers, a written report and a viva.

MA in Modern History

Course content: two core courses. 1) Historical Skills and Resources which concentrates on the nature and location of resources, bibliographical and library skills, plus foreign languages, computing and palaeography skills according to request. 2) State and Society: historical concepts and problems: eight seminars per term, some selected by students from choices including War, State and Society, Religion and the State, Gender, Politics and the State, History as a Tool of Governance.

Assessed by short assignments and a 15,000–20,000 supervised dissertation which accounts for 60% of the final MA mark.

MSc/Diploma in Numerical Solution of Differential Equations

Course content: compulsory lectures in: Initial Value Problems, Boundary Value Problems, Differential Equation Theory, Finite Element Methods, Computing Techniques and Modelling, Applications of the Numerical Solution of Differential Equations, Industrial Modelling. Optional courses, including: Optimal Systems and Control Theory, Hydrodynamics, Asymtotic Methods, Spectral Theory and Integral Equations, Dynamical Systems, Reaction Diffusion Theory.

Assessed by written examination after the first two terms, oral examination in June and submission of dissertation by September. (Students are divided into Diploma and MSc students after the second term.)

MSc in Economics

Course content: Macroeconomic Theory and Policy, Microeconomic Theory and Policy, Methods of Economic Investigation, plus one of the following options: Advanced Economic Theory, Financial Economics, Econometrics, History of Economic Thought, Industrial Economics, Labour Economics, Monetary Economics, Public Sector Economics, Economics of Latin America, Economics of Law.

Assessed by written examination.

Why would I take an academic course?

Students normally take them because they want the chance to bury themselves in detailed study for pure enjoyment and intellectual satisfaction or because they are testing out whether or not they wish to go on further – to doctoral research.

Is that a good or bad idea? It depends on what your motivation is. Val Butcher says, 'Students must remember that if they take an academic course they will be in exactly the same position in a year's time, with exactly the same occupations to choose from. They will be a year older and a year poorer. Doing something you enjoy though can be a positive factor. If you get a real buzz from doing it you often become a more positive person, so it is not always a negative step.'

The MRes – a master's course in research

Why should I take a course in research. Isn't this built into all higher courses?

Not according to the Government. The MRes is a relatively new qualification – a master's degree in the theory and practice of research. Born as a result of the 1993 Government White Paper, *Realising our Potential*, which declared that, 'The traditional PhD is not well matched to the needs of a career outside research in academia or in an industrial research laboratory', and suggested that in due course all research students should be compelled to take one, the MRes was piloted at 23 universities, which between them had a total of 260 (official) places – although several more decided to introduce their own version, bumping up the numbers. The Government never actually made it compulsory.

Funding Councils reacted to it in different ways. Whereas the National Environmental Research Council and Office of Science and Technology funded 45 and 250 places respectively, the Economic and Social Research Council and Particle Physics and Astronomy Research Council decided against doing so, because their courses, they felt, already contained the necessary training.

Who is it for?

Although an MRes sounds like a preparation for PhD work, it is intended equally to equip students with some of the skills they would need in employment, i.e. the transferable skills required by so many employers in addition to specialist knowledge.

What does it cover?

Research methodology, survey techniques, data analysis, use of computer packages, use of the Internet and completion of a thesis are the usual topics.

At Leeds University the MRes in the Built Environment includes a career learning log. Organiser, Val Butcher says, 'Students have to record the skills and developments they acquire during each module. It forces them to ask for example, 'How are my values being influenced?' – perhaps as a result of completing a study on waste management and realising its importance to the environment. At three contact points with me during the year they are asked to consider what decisions they are now able to make; how they can relate the skills gained from the master's course to choosing a career and job applications or to going on to do a PhD. This is in addition to acquiring interrogatory skills and learning how to use static enquiry sources like computer databases.'

6 MBA COURSES

Master of Business Administration (MBA) courses are big business worldwide – in Europe, the United States, Australia and Asia. In the UK alone there are now over 100 institutions producing 7,000 graduates, covering a range of programmes tailored for specific markets. So what are they, and why should you choose one? Here is your guide to MBAs.

WHAT IS AN MBA?

The Master in Business Administration (MBA) is a postgraduate management degree programme which aims to provide a broad understanding of business and management and an in-depth knowledge of specific areas. There are also a few specialised programmes.

WHY CHOOSE AN MBA?

An MBA course is designed to prepare you for general management positions. It will not turn you into a 'super-manager' but should provide you with new management skills and techniques, develop your powers of critical and strategic thinking, and increase your depth of knowledge. It will give you a widely recognised qualification and it should increase your self-awareness and confidence.

It may also satisfy one or more of the following aims but there are no guarantees:

- to improve your job prospects
- to get a higher salary
- to help with changing your career or to change companies
- to enhance your chances for promotion

- to improve your standing within your company and protect your current employment prospects.

Is it worth it?

A recent survey of MBA graduates showed that the largest group of graduates was earning between £30,000 and £40,000 with 10% over £70,000. A third of those who stayed with their present employer improved their prospects. Many companies look very favourably on the MBA but not all are totally convinced of its value. However, with the proliferation in MBA courses, employers are increasingly concerned with where you obtained your MBA.

WHERE CAN I STUDY FOR AN MBA?

Institutions running MBA courses are scattered throughout the UK and vary considerably. There are the traditional university schools, for example the London and Manchester business schools and Cranfield School of Management, which have been running MBA courses for many years; independent management centres, for example Henley Management College and Ashridge specialising in management and business education; 'new' universities and colleges of higher education, for example Kingston University and Southampton Institute who are comparative newcomers but innovative in approach; the Open University, specialising in open and distance-learning; and Oxford and Cambridge who are only just entering the field of management education.

If you look further afield to Europe, there are one or two business schools in many European countries, including some long-established, famous schools, for example INSEAD, near Paris. In the United States there are hundreds of programmes including the famous and not so famous; while in Asia and Australia new courses are springing up rapidly.

How do I choose the best school ?

Books abound on this topic (see Chapter 16). You will not find definitive lists of 'best' courses however. One way to narrow down a choice is to act on personal recommendation. You can also:

- apply all the questions suggested in Chapter 8, Choosing an Institution
- consider applying to those given accreditation by various organisations.

Accreditation

Under accreditation schemes some courses are recognised by particular bodies or associations as providing courses at a reasonable standard. This gives you some assurance of quality and, where there are a lot of courses to choose from, it can help to narrow down your options. However, these courses may not be suitable for you for a variety of reasons. You may also wish to make up your own mind and test the ambience and culture of business schools as well as weighing up their course content, specialisations, facilities etc.

The US has a system of accreditation for courses and the European Federation for Management Development (EFMD) is trying to establish some common quality standards for Europe. In the UK there is no formal 'accreditation' but the Association of MBAs (AMBA) sets criteria for membership. Their criteria for membership cover a variety of factors such as the size and strength of the faculty, the facilities, the curriculum, the staff, the student body, the admissions standards and methods of examination. Currently 32 out of the 100 or so institutions in the UK running MBAs (including four distance learning programmes) are accredited by AMBA. They also accredit twelve schools in Europe. However, AMBA does not rank the schools as it is difficult to judge whether one school is 'better' than another.

If you need to finance your own course, choosing an AMBA accredited course can be advantageous. Loan providers are often more amenable to providing finance for these.

Another measure of standards in the UK is provided by the Association of Business Schools' (ABS) subsidiary body, the Management Verification Consortium (MVC), which awards NVQs and SVQs in management at approved business schools.

SHOULD I STUDY FULL TIME OR PART TIME?

The MBA is very demanding academically. It requires total commitment to study and ideally an intensive full time course may be the best solution. This gives you the best chance to get to grips with the course, interact with the other students and successfully pass the examinations.

However, one or two years away from work is a considerable investment in time and money. It depends on factors such as how much time you feel you can afford to spend in studying, how your studies will fit in with your present family commitments and your lifestyle, how much you can financially afford both in any one year and overall, whether you can expect any help or support from your present employer. Only you can assess your individual circumstances and weigh up the pros and cons.

One of the criticisms leveled against the one year course is that it is too intensive and theoretical, but this may be offset by your previous work experience and by practical experience during the course using case studies, simulations and role play.

How long are the courses?

Most full time courses in the UK and Europe last for about one year, although there are still two year full time courses at the London Business School, IESE (University of Navarra Barcelona), ESADE (private business school in Barcelona), Helsinki and Rotterdam. In the United States the two year course is still the norm.

Part time study is the most popular option. About 80% of UK students study by this route. (This figure includes those using distance learning.) Part time courses offer more flexibility of study and will normally spread your course over at least two or three years. They enable you to carry on working, and you may well find that your studies are directly helpful in your present job. But time-management will be a problem – your free time will be virtually non-existent and you will probably also find that you are unable or unwilling to put the extra hours into your present job which you or/and your employer feel it needs. So developing your present job, seeking out new challenges at work and promotion prospects are likely to go on hold for several years.

It is worth checking whether you can change to a different mode of study if your circumstances change, but whatever route you choose you will need good motivation.

How can I study part time?

Part time study can be by various modes – evening, weekends, day-release, block release, or distance or open learning. Part time courses are generally the same as the full time version – they just take longer to complete. Most include at least a one-week residential period.

Modular MBAs are a bit like sandwich courses, alternating college-based study with practical project work in the workplace. Since they incorporate periods of full time study they may last only 18 months although two years is normal.

'Distance-learning' or 'Open Learning' MBA programmes are becoming increasingly important and the number of courses is expanding rapidly. By 1996 the Open University alone expected to produce 20 per cent of all UK MBA graduates! Distance-learning or open learning are simply the up-market names for correspondence courses, with the major difference being that open learning courses usually include at least some mandatory attendance at college. They normally take about three years to complete. Many of them are taking advantage of advances in information technology using video conferencing and the Internet. They are offered at a handful of colleges including Durham, Heriot-Watt, Nottingham, Warwick, Kingston and Oxford Brookes Universities, Henley Management College and the Open Business School (Open University). Most programmes have a modular structure and students can often follow a personalised study route. The drop-out rate is high.

IS MY EMPLOYER LIKELY TO SPONSOR ME?

Employers are unlikely to sponsor you on a full time course and most students on these are predominantly self-funded. You may have more chance on a part time MBA programme and two thirds of students are supported by their employers in some way, i.e. they are full or partially financed, allowed study leave, etc. You need to ensure that the employer is fully committed to supporting you for the duration of the course and that you have the support of your line manager who will arrange cover in your absence.

Students are more likely to be sponsored on the following part time programmes:

- Modular MBA courses. (These would be difficult to complete without some co-operation from an employer.)
- Executive MBAs lasting for two to three years are perceived as courses for high-fliers. Study is usually at weekends and students have to be sponsored.
- In-Company MBAs are tailored to a particular company's needs. Such courses are constantly being developed. One of the newest on the scene is one timed to start this year, designed by IBM in conjunction with the Manchester Business School. In-house courses will obviously be highly regarded by your own company but you may miss out on the stimulus gained from interacting with other students and you may find that your course is not highly regarded by other employers.
- Consortium MBAs are designed by a group of 3–6 companies

specifically to meet the needs of those companies. They can have a valuable mix of students. For example, the Consortium MBA at Lancaster University has a mix of industry, the public sector and privatised utilities.

The obvious first step if you are contemplating an MBA course is to find out if your employer is already committed to a particular type of MBA course and what selection criteria they use to decide who is sent on them.

WHAT DO THE COURSES COVER?

A generalist MBA programme usually covers a number of compulsory core subjects in basic business disciplines which take up to about two-thirds of the timetable, plus a number of optional or elective subjects. Core subjects include accounting and statistics, business finance, human resource management, organisational behaviour, marketing, business policy, economics, and information technology. Some schools also provide refresher courses in basic mathematics.

The elective courses either continue with more general studies or allow you to specialise in a particular area such as environmental issues, languages, creative management, interviewing skills, managing public services, etc. Electives may be taken abroad.

Options might include advanced marketing, global strategy, industrial market analysis or production management.

Course content varies but most will include case studies, role play and simulations. Some courses teach subjects in an integrated way, showing the relationships between the various disciplines. Many courses include a project or/and dissertation which may be carried out within a company.

Could I specialise on an MBA?

Most MBAs are generalist programmes with a choice of electives which give some degree of specialisation. However, there are a few specialist MBAs. For example, some courses have an international focus (for example at City, Exeter, Greenwich, Chicago or Rotterdam); or a health focus (for example at Durham, Glasgow, Keele or Berkeley); a housing focus (Glasgow); oil industry (Dundee); or agribusiness (Royal Agricultural College or Aberystwyth).

ENTRY REQUIREMENTS

The minimum entry requirement is usually a first degree in any subject, or the equivalent, plus at least two years' quality work experience. For those without a degree, a minimum of five years' work experience at a significant level of achievement is required. If you are interested in a postgraduate management education course and you have only recently graduated then you should consider a specialist MSc programme rather than an MBA.

However, applicants outnumber places so business schools use a battery of selection criteria to assess your work experience; your motivation, commitment and enthusiasm; your personal qualities; your quantitative skills and communication skills. Selection tests may include the Graduate Management Admission Test (GMAT).

What is the GMAT test?

The GMAT is an American test lasting four hours, testing verbal and quantitative skills (problem solving, reading comprehension, writing skill, analytical proficiency and critical reasoning). It is offered four times a year in October, January, March and June and can be taken at several places in the UK. It is advisable to take it as early as possible. Details are given in the GMAT *Bulletin of Information* or in business school prospectuses. There is a fee of $80 for taking the test.

It was developed in the United States where business school admissions staff felt in need of an objective test that would counterbalance discrepancies in grades awarded to students coming from different colleges. Its purpose is to add an objective assessment to grades, interviews and references, all of which are used in selecting students. GMAT, therefore, is designed to measure your ability to think systematically and to employ reading and analytical skills. It does not test specific knowledge. You are expected to have a knowledge of basic arithmetic, algebra and geometry however!

GMAT is used by almost all US business schools and widely accepted throughout the rest of the world. Scores range from 200 – 800. For UK business schools 500 is probably the absolute minimum but many look for between 550 and 650.

Some schools use their own tests which are very similar to GMAT for testing numeracy, literacy and verbal and numerical reasoning.

HOW DO I APPLY FOR A COURSE?

AMBA acts as a clearing house for enquiries from those contemplating starting an MBA but there is no central applications procedure.

There is no common application form and applications have to be made direct to the business school. You should fill in the application form very carefully, and send it off early as places, scholarships and bursaries tend to be allocated on a first-come, first-served basis. Unofficial advice is to only apply to three schools. There is an application fee for each course of between £25–£40 so it can be expensive to apply to too many!

For courses starting September/October, application deadlines are April/May.

WHAT WILL IT COST TO DO AN MBA?

An MBA course is expensive. Tuition fees alone for full time courses at business schools in the UK can cost between £6,000 and

£11,000. Living costs are additional. Fees for top European schools such as INSEAD in France are 145,000 French francs, or at IESE, 1,960,000 pesetas!

Where can I get the money to pay for the course?

From various sources – which are covered in Chapter 11. There are comparatively few bursaries and scholarships however. If you were lucky you might be sponsored by an employer. AMBA operates a business loan scheme for courses 'accredited' by them in the UK, Europe and US. Their average loan for studying abroad is £23,467 for courses on the Continent and £36,000 for studying in the USA.

Many students have to finance themselves through Career Development Loans or by other means.

See Chapter 11 for more information on financing your course.

WHERE CAN I OBTAIN MORE INFORMATION?

- Attend a business fair.
  AMBA run a Business School Fair in London each October; the University of London organises a similar one in February.

- Write to:
  Association of Business Schools (ABS)
  Association of Masters in Business Administration (AMBA)
- Surf the Internet.
- Send off for prospectuses.

CHECKLIST OF QUESTIONS TO ASK

- What does the course include?
- How large is the school?
- What is its culture?
- How good are the facilities?

- Is it international in outlook? (i.e. exchanges with other countries, learning a foreign language)
- What is its position in published surveys and rankings?
- Is the course accredited?
- What are the success and failure rates?
- What is the job placement record?

7 TEACHING AND LEARNING

Before you make the decision between the different types of course you'll need to know a bit more about what you might be letting yourself in for.

HOW ARE THEY ORGANISED?

Diplomas and certificates

Diploma and certificate courses last for six to twelve months, depending on the subject. Topics studied may include some modules from taught courses taken by MBA and MA/MSc students. Work experience placements or short attachments to observe work in a particular profession are often included. Courses do not normally include a dissertation, although at some institutions there is the opportunity to convert the qualification into a master's, through completion of a dissertation or project.

Taught Master's Degrees

These usually take nine to twelve months (or two years if you are a part time student). The first six to nine months normally consist of lectures, tutorials, seminars and practicals, as in undergraduate programmes. In most cases this period is followed by time spent on a research project. The amount of time allowed for the project varies in different universities and colleges. On some courses two terms of lectures and other work such as practicals are followed by examinations. A diploma is then awarded. After acceptance of a dissertation the master's degree is awarded.

The dissertation is research-based and although it is not as long as a doctoral thesis (most dissertations are about 10,000 words), writing it gives you the chance to find out whether you like research work and whether a doctorate might be a suitable next step. Students on science and technological courses may do a supervised project – often in industry.

What would the weekly workload be?

It varies. However, on many courses the pattern is to have about six hours of formal teaching – lectures and seminars – with additional time for practicals, problem classes etc. As at undergraduate level, the time can vary according to whether you are on a humanities or science course. Some science students have as many as 24 hours of taught time each week with lab work on top.

On the MSc/Diploma course in Sedimentology and its Applications for example, whose admissions tutor Professor Bruce Sellwood provides some guidance on applications in Chapter 10, the first half of the course from October consists mainly of taught courses, lab work and about five study visit days. The taught element amounts to between 15–24 contact hours a week. May onwards is dissertation time. Students sort out their dissertation subject in discussions with the staff, then have to write around 7,000 words by the end of August. Some students choose to work abroad and have transported themselves to Southern Spain, Corsica, Mombasa and Barbados. But most are UK based and some choose to work in the labs at Reading.

Some humanities students, in contrast, have as little as three hours of lectures and seminars. Seminars are like those at undergraduate level, revolving around a paper prepared and presented by one student. Lecturers often read their papers too. Postgraduate education is also moving in the direction of set projects and assignments with students working in small groups and reporting back to the whole group. Teaching groups are usually smaller than those on undergraduate courses.

You should also receive some individual tuition.

Obviously, there is a lot of individual reading to be done. Jonathan Lestor (see page 127) who is doing a philosophy course, estimates that he reads and prepares essays for 20 hours per week.

How would I be assessed?

Assessment methods now vary widely. There has been a slight swing away from traditional examinations, although these still exist and are still the main method at some institutions. You could be assessed by any one or any combination of the following:

- written examination
- coursework
- a number of long essays – up to 5,000 words long
- an oral or 'viva'.

RESEARCH PROGRAMMES

How do these differ from taught courses?

In the majority of cases the student chooses the topic of research. He or she then submits a proposal to an institution and is accepted. Some research posts however are advertised. They are tempting because they come with funding attached. You would have to be very sure however, that the topic really did interest you. Sometimes advertisements are made for a researcher to join an established project and work on a part of it. In such cases the thesis (which still has to be original) is composed from that part alone.

Most research students work without receiving very much formal instruction, although most doctorates include some course work. The main thrust of a doctorate is the thesis, prepared under the guidance and support of a supervisor, whom students should meet on a regular basis. (The supervisor is a member of departmental staff whose research is in a similar field.)

Although these degrees are awarded for the completion of a piece of research rather than attendance at courses, the initial part of the course – several months – often concentrates on the acquisition of necessary skills and techniques: analytical techniques, information technology and computing etc. (These are the same skills as those taught in the new MRes courses.) The student then moves on to original research and is normally expected to produce an outline/list of objectives/progress report by the end of the first year. The doctoral thesis of 80,000–100,000 words is expected to be an original work which makes a definite contribution to knowledge. The topic of the thesis needs careful consideration (as does the choice of a supervisor).

Even if some course work features on the programme the doctorate is usually awarded solely on the thesis – which the student has to defend during a compulsory viva.

The MPhil thesis generally has a maximum of 60,000 words and is not required to reach the same level of originality as a doctorate.

Students often register first for an MPhil then transfer to a PhD programme.

There are also some one and two year Master's by Research programmes. Students attend lectures – which may include those on any appropriate postgraduate or undergraduate course and also submit a dissertation.

Last, a few institutions now offer taught doctorates. They are rather like the taught masters but longer – three or four years – and culminate in a thesis (up to 40,000 words). These programmes exist largely in vocational areas such as engineering, clinical psychology or engineering.

What about the workload?

The workload on all research programmes is considerable – but in most cases decided by the individual student. Science students are often assigned to a research group – typically consisting of members of academic staff, research assistants and research students – so some group decisions regarding working practices have to be made.

How do I choose a topic?

The choice would be up to you, the student, but a proposal for it must be submitted to the department you wish to join. Any funding body giving you assistance must also approve it.

HOW DO PEOPLE CHOOSE BETWEEN TAUGHT AND RESEARCH PROGRAMMES?

By personal inclination. There is a great deal of difference in the methods of work. Do you like working alone with the assistance of a supervisor or do you prefer some class contact with academic staff and with other students? Points to consider include:

- personal interests
- aims – both personal and in career terms
- subject of first degree and intended progression
- time available
- financial situation.

To sum up

	Postgraduate Certificate or Diploma	MSc/MA/MBA
Is	a taught course	a taught course, also known as a higher degree by instruction
Takes	one year full time two years part time	one to two years full time two to three years part time
Requires for entry	a degree	minimum lower second
Is awarded on	examination	examination plus dissertation/thesis

	MPhil	PhD/DPhil
Is	a higher degree by research	a higher degree by research
Takes	two to three years full time four to five years part time	three to four years full time five to six years part time
Requires for entry	minimum upper second	minimum upper second or master's degree
Is awarded on	thesis plus oral examination	thesis plus oral examination.

Checklist of questions to ask

- Do I need to take an MRes before proceding to my research programme?
- How many class contact hours are there?
- How often would I meet my supervisor?
- Could I change course/supervisor if necessary?
- Is it easy to convert from a MPhil to PhD?
- Is the course approved by appropriate professional bodies?
- Can postgraduates use the careers advisory service?

8 CHOOSING A COURSE – AND WHERE TO DO IT

What should I study?

You will choose a course for all sorts of reasons, many of which are outlined in other chapters. You will probably want to consult all the sources of advice available to you before making a final decision. These include:

- Current tutor – who knows your ability.
- Other members of teaching staff in your current department, who know your particular strengths.
- Possible employers in a career field that interests you.
- Careers advisers.

Your tutor

If you have enjoyed a good relationship with your personal tutor during your degree course, he or she should know your ability and be able to advise on what level of higher course you would be capable of – not to mention your ability to meet deadlines and hand work in on time.

Lecturers

If you are hoping to continue in a specialist field within your first degree subject or in a closely related area, then subject lecturers should also be able to guide you. They will be able to help with the sort of course you should be aiming for and will know the sort of research and teaching carried out in other departments throughout the country, in addition to what happens in your own university or college.

Both the above are good sources of advice and information on academic courses.

One person who is often asked for advice is Professor John Macklin, Head of the Department of Spanish and Portuguese at Leeds University. The department gives all final year students a handbook which explains all the options available to them, advises them to consult the careers advisory service and also offers any would be postgraduate student the opportunity to talk to a member of staff who will advise on courses – at Leeds and elsewhere.

What are the issues normally discussed? Professor Macklin says, 'We establish with them first whether they are clear about the different patterns of postgraduate study and the range of courses available. It is important for them to be aware that funding for postgraduate study in the humanities is very difficult to get. Very many students are self-funding and many study part time. The main source of funding is the Humanities Research Board which runs two competitions. Competition A is for a one year award, usually for a taught master's course with a research and methodology element, although funding can be awarded for a tailor-made course of study prior to undertaking doctoral research. Competition B is for three year awards to undertake such research. The Board has effectively moved to a 1+3 model in which funding for a three year period of research is very difficult to obtain without one year's previous postgraduate study. Most universities do offer their own bursaries, as do individual departments. Another pattern which has become more common in recent years is for a student to be employed as a teaching assistant and register for a higher degree part time.

'In choosing the course they need to be especially careful. There are so many master's programmes now, all with different emphases. They need to look very closely at the course content. If asked for advice, I would want to know why they wanted to do a course, what they hoped to get out of it – and might suggest particular places. An example might be a student interested in courses in Latin America.

These students should certainly look at the Institutes of Latin American Studies, such as those in London or Liverpool, and in Leeds we offer a multidisciplinary MA in Contemporary Ibero-American Studies.'

Journals and Surveys

If you are considering a research degree, you could also look in academic journals to see what research is being carried out in various places.

Where vocational courses are concerned, you could look for copies of surveys conducted by the Association of Graduate Careers Advisory Services (AGCAS). Individual surveys summarise course information under the following headings:

Institution
Course title
Duration
Course tutor
Number of places
Number of applications
When full? (i.e. apply before . . .)
Fees (1994/5)
How financed
Selection criteria
Number of current students over 25 years old
Number of jobs gained within six months of the end of the course
Employment fields entered
Comments from course director.

A sample entry from one of the universities offering a Postgraduate Diploma in Business and Management Studies reads as follows:

Duration   8½ months
Course tutor

Number of places	24
Number of applications	50
When full? (i.e. apply before . . .)	October
Fees (1994/5)	£3,055 full time, (£5,900 overseas students) £1,250 part time
How financed	Self funded; Career Development Loan
Selection criteria	Degree or HND
Number of students over 25 years old	33%
Number of jobs gained within six months of the end of the course	50%
Employment fields entered	Various. Financial brokerage, contracts management, financial analysis, human resources, lecturing, NHS management.
Comments from course director	Course includes one week in Europe and other international links. Gives membership of Institute of Marketing. Many students continue to MBA courses.

Surveys, which should be available for reference at your careers service, have been completed on: *Accountancy, Counselling, Film, Visual and Sound Media, Health Therapies and Nursing, Information Technology and Information Engineering, Journalism, Language Translation and Interpreting, Library and Information Management, Personnel Management, Printing and Publishing, RSA Certificate in TEFL, Secretarial Work, Youth and Community Work,* plus *LEA Discretionary Awards for Postgraduate Courses* (all 1994); *Careers Guidance, Cartography, Land Surveying & Geographical Information Systems, Diplomas in Business and Management Studies, Environmental Management and Conservation, Heritage Management and Museum Work, Hotel and Hospitality*

Management, Housing and Property Management, Landscape Architecture, Marketing, Advertising and Public Relations, Master of Business Administration, Operational Research, Tourism, Leisure and Recreation. Town and Regional Planning, Transport and Distribution (1995).

Fairs

If a postgraduate fair is being held anywhere near you this year, do try to go. It should give you the chance to talk to representatives from different universities and colleges about their courses.

Employers

At some point you are going to have to hit the employment market. It is a sad fact that no postgraduate qualification guarantees you a job, even though it can enhance your prospects. Nor does possession of one automatically lead to an academic career. It can therefore be useful to try out the value of your proposed qualification on a sample of employers. This does not mean writing hundreds of letters. You probably would not get many replies in any case. But you could attend some of the employer presentations likely to be made to final year students by representatives from various organisations and ask then. You could also attend any recruitment fairs being held and speak to a selection of company representatives.

Job advertisements in national newspapers and the academic press could also give you an insight into possible employment opportunities for people with your intended qualification.

Careers advice

This is something that nobody should omit before enrolling for any postgraduate course. The careers advisory service at your institution does not exist merely to guide finalists into suitable employment. The staff can talk through all your ideas with you and help to weigh up the merits of various options, postgraduate study included. Some services have advisers who specialise in advising postgraduates and prospective postgraduate students. More common is for careers advisers to work with students on a number of courses. They are therefore expert in all the possibilities that degrees and diplomas in 'their' subjects can lead to.

Roger Brown has had considerable experience in advising under-graduates, whatever their slant. He is now the Deputy Director of Reading University's Careers Advisory Service and currently helps to plan the future of students taking economics, management studies, computer science, law, English, and until recently history. His caseload is around 400 final year students in total.

Part of Roger's role is to help students to decide on postgraduate courses. At Reading, 1995 figures show 16.2 per cent taking this route, compared with 57 per cent going into employment – including temporary work – and 5.2 per cent still job hunting. This shows a downturn in the postgraduate option, but Roger says it's largely because of the cash shortage. There's been no real improvement in the employment situation.

Roger helps students look at their reasons for considering the postgraduate route. Is it pure interest in the subject or will it have a direct impact on their career choice? He also guides them through the maze of options of taught Master's, MPhil and doctoral programmes and vocational diplomas and certificates. He says,

'Some students are unclear about what is most appropriate. A student looking for a research degree needs to talk to a tutor to see if they are the right sort of person. It suits the highly motivated, well organised person, as it can be a rather long and lonely road and one needs a lot of stamina to see it through. Some students will take a Master's course first then move on to a PhD, but it's often better to go straight to the PhD.'

Students often ask advice on the 'best place' for a particular course. 'Again that's a difficult one. HEFC quality assessments of courses exist, but there's a certain scepticism about their usefulness. Advice from academic staff is of variable quality. Views of former students or potential employers on the usefulness of a course can be most helpful.'

Roger provided a few specific examples of advice about further study. Law students will find that funding for the Legal Practice Course (LPC) and obtaining a training contract are difficult. Some say, 'I don't know whether it's worth the candle.' The would-be lawyer may occasionally find a sympathetic local education authority, obtain a scholarship from a city solicitor, raid the family funds or take out a career development loan. But they are not advised to start the LPC course unless a training contract is lined up. So Roger's job is often to advise on other career options. On this list are the City and corporate banking, tax consultancy, personnel, the Civil Service fast stream and the European fast stream.

Like Roger, Ann Henderson from King Alfred's College in Winchester often has to advise students to consider several possibilities in case funding doesn't materialise. 'Do check the funding situation. It is no good thinking about this at the last minute. Funding can be a "chicken and egg" scenario in that you have to get your place before you can apply for funding! BUT this does not stop you exploring the options and planning the way ahead should you be successful in your application for a course. You will need more than one idea as funding is so difficult that it is advisable to be well prepared and to have more than one possibility in mind.'

YOU HAVE CHOSEN A COURSE. WHERE SHOULD YOU DO IT?

There are all sorts of reasons for choosing one institution rather than another, including personal and social reasons, financial factors and location.

Is it a good idea to stay at the same university, always assuming that they do the course?

There are points for and against.

On the plus side for staying are:

- familiarity with the work of the department
- good relationships with staff already established
- friends may be staying on
- you know the area and where to look for accommodation (or may be able to retain your present accommodation).

Going elsewhere can:

- give you the chance to meet different people
- enable you to experience different teaching styles.
- demonstrate your flexibility and ease in adapting to new circumstances – which often impresses employers.

You will also want to consider the reputation of the course you are intending to take and the quality of the department.

Quality

There has been concern that many of the new master's programmes that have been established are little different from undergraduate courses in the teaching methods used and often consist of modules taken from various undergraduate programmes. This may be fine for conversion courses but not for a student genuinely wanting a higher level of specialist study. Unlike some countries, Britain does not differentiate between different levels of master's programmes. In Australia for instance, postgraduate courses are classified as **broadening** or **deepening** knowledge.

How do I assess a department's reputation?

This is not always easy because reputations come and go. Tied in as they are with the work of the departmental staff, they can soon become outdated. Two experts in a particular topic go elsewhere and suddenly the expertise is gone. Advice needs to be up to date. Hearsay too can be a very unreliable source of information. Personal recommendation from someone who really knows on the other hand is invaluable. Use all the sources of information already outlined above.

In addition, you may or may not know that there are various forms of organised inspection and quality control which have given individual departments quality ratings after an assessment. They are not infallible and some departments view them with suspicion, pointing out that evaluations quickly become dated. Nevertheless, departments that have received favourable reports are usually quite quick to quote from them in their prospectuses. Reports are published and are accessible.

The Higher Education Funding Councils (HEFCs)

They produce reports on individual subjects, after assessing a department's research and teaching standards. For research, grades are awarded from 1–5, with 5A being given if every subject within a department is at quality level 5. Teaching is assessed by looking at teaching methods, facilities and examination results, and taking into account students' views and the views of employers who have recruited students from that institution. Grades are given as Excellent, Satisfactory or Unsatisfactory.

To date, the following subjects (taught courses) have been assessed: anthropology, applied social work, architecture, business and management studies, chemistry, computer studies, English, environmental studies, French, geography, geology, history, Iberian studies, law, mechanical engineering, music, Russian, social policy and administration, sociology.

How are the assessments made?

The four HEFCs (England, Northern Ireland, Scotland and Wales) require self assessment reports from institutions. Teams at each

Council then do a desk assessment which is followed by visits during which assessors observe lectures, seminars, tutorials and workshops, inspect facilities and examine syllabuses, coursework, projects and dissertations. They also talk to students and staff. The number of visits made varies. The HEFCs for Scotland and Wales for example do a follow up visit to every institution. The HEFC for England visits about fifty per cent.

Overview reports of each subject are then published.

You can obtain a copy of each subject overview (which gives information on the teaching of the subject but restricts information on individual institutions to the grades), or of the individual assessments from the HEFCs – but they should also be available for consultation in your library and are on the Internet.

Research Assessment Exercise (RAE)

This body assesses postgraduate research. Seventy-two subject areas are assessed and rated from 1–5. The primary aim of the assessments is to allocate research resources. For departmental allocations 95 per cent of research funding is based on the RAE assessments. Currently the majority of funding is concentrated in the following universities (in descending order): London, Oxford, Cambridge, Edinburgh, Glasgow, Manchester, Birmingham, Bristol, Southampton, Liverpool, Leeds, Newcastle, Nottingham, Sheffield, Leicester, Strathclyde.

Since one of the major aspects assessed is staff and their publications, this information will be the most helpful if you are considering a research degree; it will give you an idea of the standard of research in a specific department. To view the December 1996 survey on the Internet visit http://www.niss.ac.uk/education/hefc/rae96/

How do I interpret the assessment grades?

They follow an international five point scale, defined as follows:

1. Research quality that equates to attainable levels of national excellence in none, or virtually none, of the sub-areas of activity.
2. Research quality that equates to attainable levels of national excellence in up to half of the sub-areas of activity.
3. Research quality that equates to attainable levels of national excellence in a majority of the sub-areas of activity, or to international level in some.
4. Research quality that equates to attainable levels of national excellence in virtually all sub-areas of activity, possibly showing some evidence of international excellence, or to international level in some and at least national level in a majority.
5. Research quality that equates to attainable levels of international excellence in some sub-areas of activity and to attainable levels of national excellence in virtually all others.

Internal audits

Even before the existence of the HEFCs and RAE, universities and colleges were all responsible for maintaining standards – and still are. All set their own aims and have some kind of quality control system to make sure that individual departments are achieving them. The Higher Education Quality Council, which is supported by the institutions, checks that these internal systems are working properly.

The HEFCE, CVCP, SCOP review of postgraduate education (the Harris Review)

This review was set up on behalf of the Committee of Vice-Chancellors and Principals, the Higher Education Funding Council for England (HEFCE) and the Standing Conference of Principals. The committee examined all levels of postgraduate courses. It had a wide-ranging remit but one of its considerations was, 'What are the main "drivers" for expansion in the number of postgraduate courses?' Answers were sought from students, employers and institutions. Where the institutions are concerned, questions included: Is the growth in postgraduate courses

- a response to the increased pool of qualified applicants?
- to meet the needs of the economy?
- to develop the research mission and contribute to scholarship or the stock of knowledge?

Or –

- to increase numbers of students to gain additional funding
- to reap economies of scale in provision?

In answering these questions the Review considered the 'Institutional provision of postgraduate study and its quality.' It has considered the full range of postgraduate education, including research and taught provision in all modes and subject areas. For a copy of the Review, contact the HEFCE External Relations department on 0117 931 7317.

Vocational courses

The AGCAS surveys mentioned earlier, while not being concerned with evaluating quality of teaching or research, do contain information on the range of employment fields entered by students leaving courses and the percentages gaining employment within six months of leaving. As far as quality of vocational qualifications is concerned, the success rate in finding suitable employment has to be a good indication!

Special points for intending research students

Every research student has a supervisor who directs their project. If you are planning to do a research degree you must find a supervisor. He or she is going to be very important to you. You will have to work closely together for the coming years. It is to your supervisor you will go for advice and discussion. It is important to choose a supervisor whom you like and can relate to.

How do I choose a supervisor?

- Use all the available sources to establish which department you wish to apply to and to find out the research interests of the members of staff (prospectuses, *Current Research in Britain* etc).
- Read some of their publications.
- Make your applications and discuss potential supervisors at interview (unless you have already made an informal approach). NB It is not always a good idea to choose a famous name. The person you select may spend more time delivering conference papers around the globe than at the home university.

Before you accept the offer of a supervisor you need to know:

- What is his/her area of specialist research?
- What are his or her recent publications?
- Is he or she used to supervising students?

So far it sounds as though all the choice is on your side! But you have to be accepted by a supervisor too. You may want to work with someone who already feels they have too many students to supervise and does not want any more. When you receive the offer of a place it will usually name your supervisor and the project you are going to work on. The choice of supervisor should have been made by mutual agreement.

CHECKLIST OF QUESTIONS TO ASK

- How many staff are there in the department?
- How many other postgraduate students?
- What are the research interests of staff and students?
- What are my prospective supervisor's interests?
- Is he or she experienced in supervising students?
- Will he/she be there – or away on lecture tours/ sabbatical? If so, does the department undertake to provide a substitute?
- Can my work be published? (Useful to put on a CV!)

- Does the department have bursaries available?
- How did the various quality assessments rate it?
- What are the library, computing facilities etc?
- Which facilities are still available during the vacations?

9 WHEN TO DO A POSTGRADUATE COURSE

DO I HAVE TO GO STRAIGHT ON TO A HIGHER DEGREE COURSE?

No, not necessarily. It depends on your reason for wanting to do one. If you want to pursue an aspect of your first degree in more depth, then it probably is the right thing to go straight on, while the interest is still burning. But if you are torn between postgraduate study and a job offer **and** the job does not require further qualifications, it can make sense to wait. You might re-evaluate after a few years in employment; might have a different course in mind. You will be in a better position to afford a postgraduate course if you have been able to save. Alternatively you might decide to study on a part time basis.

The decision is often made on the basis of financial support available – and can sometimes be made quite late in the year. Often, the crucial letter about funding doesn't come until quite late in the summer. As students quite frequently feel they cannot take further money from their families, it's common to work for a year, then return to the academic world. It is also increasingly common for students to take a master's degree part time over a two year period.

STUDY WHILE IN EMPLOYMENT

Many students study for a postgraduate qualification while they are in employment – with the support and/or encouragement of their employers. For some courses work experience is seen as a valuable contribution, if not a prerequisite for entry. Because of these factors, students on some courses may be older than the typical recent graduate. As far as the MBA is concerned for example, most UK courses look for at least three years work experience. From an age point of view the average age of those on full time courses is between 25 and 29 and for those on part time courses between 35 and 39. Recent job adverts for MBA graduates have specified an age range of around 26–38.

CAN I RETURN TO STUDY AS A MATURE STUDENT?

Why not?

Mature students make up ever increasing numbers on postgraduate courses. They also form a significant proportion of those studying through distance learning. You will have to look very carefully into the finance question of course, especially if you are considering taking a full time course. The demands of employer or family will have to be taken into account if you are thinking of part time study. You may also be constrained by geographical factors and consequent lack of mobility. For all these reasons, distance learning may well prove to be the preferred option.

Will selectors give me any special consideration?

They are unlikely to reduce their standard academic criteria for academic courses, namely the requirement for an upper second for some courses – but the additional experience and expertise you should bring to the course if you have been in related employment should count in your favour. You may also find that thanks to CATS (see Chapter 4) you can negotiate some credits towards the award. Where gaining admission to vocational courses is concerned, previous experience can count for a great deal.

You will certainly be made welcome however and, given the varied ages of students undertaking postgraduate study, you should not feel like a fish out of water, even on a full time course. Mature students have the reputation of being very committed to their subject. After all, they frequently make considerable sacrifices in order to be able to pursue it.

Some of the profiles in this book are of mature students. Some of them talk about the particular difficulties they have faced.

CHECKLIST OF QUESTIONS TO ASK

Current undergraduates

- How can the timing of a course fit in with my career plans?
- If I wanted to take some time off after graduating (say to travel) could I manage to complete all the forms/attend interviews?
- Do I need to spend some time gaining experience before I can apply for a course?

Mature students

- Will it be easy to get back into employment if I leave in order to do a full time course?
- Could I do this programme on a part time basis?
- How many mature students are on the course?
- Will I find return to academic study difficult?
- Is there any special preparatory course I could take?
- Is there a creche?

Part time students

- What time of day or evening are lectures?
- Does the course involve attendance at any weekend sessions?
- Can I realistically fit this in with my job?
- Is my employer going to be flexible if I need to take days off to attend special sessions?

10 MAKING APPLICATIONS

HOW DO I APPLY FOR A COURSE?

After the comparatively straightforward UCAS system you are used to, the method of application for postgraduate courses is initially rather confusing – as are sources of information. Open days exist but are often patchy for postgraduate students.

Application does not take place at specific dates for all courses. Some taught programmes have deadlines, and of course these must be observed. For research programmes admission does not necessarily take place on set dates.

There may be different starting dates throughout the year for all types of courses – but the autumn term is still the most popular starting date and other courses often follow term dates, often starting after Christmas. A suggested timetable to observe is given at the end of the chapter.

How many applications should I make?

This is partly a matter of personal choice and depends on where you would like to go. It also depends on the popularity of the course you choose. You may want to maximise your chances of acceptance by applying to several. Ask advice.

Most students need to make around six applications maximum and on average around two to three.

For MBA courses, general advice is – three applications. This seems particularly sensible in view of the fact that there is a not inconsiderable fee for each application! (See chapter 6).

How do I do this?

It depends on the course you want.

- An application form is the usual method.
- But in some cases a written letter is expected instead.
- For some courses, for example, law, teacher training, social work, an application form is required but it comes from a central clearing house (like UCAS) and must be returned there.

Where do I get the application forms?

Again that depends on the course. For the majority it means individual applications – and few forms are identical. Each university and college devises its own. You might have to fill in quite different ones for similar courses. You obtain these on request from an institution's postgraduate office.

Applications to the courses handled by the centralised application systems are made on standard forms obtained from the individual clearing house.

In all cases, the first step is to write to the postgraduate admissions offices at a number of institutions to ask for prospectuses, course leaflets, application forms (if issued) and details of any available funding, and/or to the appropriate clearing house.

Then, remembering that you are a customer (hard as this may seem when you feel desperate to get a place!), you will want to find out as much as you can about the institution, the course, facilities and so on. Informal approaches – letters and visits – are in order, in fact positively encouraged.

Most departments welcome visits from prospective students. Where research degrees are concerned this is particularly relevant. Michael Lea, Professor of Physics at Royal Holloway College, London University, says, 'No department should refuse a request for a visit. Make one, look around, talk to academic staff – especially those engaged in your line of research and potential supervisors. Equally important, talk to postgraduate students already there. Get them to show you round. Ask questions.' One particularly important aspect, he says, is to find out which projects the different research teams are doing and which group you might be able to join.

THE APPLICATION FORM

Are there any tips for completing this?

Yes, there are the usual ones applicable to any application form:

- Read the form thoroughly before you start to write anything.
- Take photocopies and do several practice drafts.
- Use black ink (to make the form easier to photocopy at the other end).
- Include all the facts that will support your application. Sell yourself.
- Make sure you have your referee's permission before giving his or her name.
- If you are asked to enclose any samples of work, make sure that you follow to the letter instructions regarding length, subject matter and so on.

Remember the advice you had from your school on completing a UCAS form two or three years ago? Dig it out from the depths of your memory!

What sort of questions can I expect?

All the usual personal and academic details. There will probably be one on funding too. Institutions are particularly anxious to find out whether you have any sources or whether you will be asking them for assistance. Then there will be the more tricky ones, designed to establish whether you are a suitable person for the proposed course.

Sample questions taken from a genuine application form:

- Career you intend to follow after completing the course.
- Financial support. Give details of your proposed source of funding. (Show here that you have investigated these. Give the name of the funding source, if any, and enclose photocopied details of offers of support. If it is going to be a bank loan or family, say how much money you have been guaranteed.)
- Give details of any professional, industrial or research experience relevant to your application. In particular, applicants for post-experience programmes (e.g. Education, the MBA, Social Work) should complete this section as fully as possible. (Give details of any relevant work experience, paid or voluntary and describe any visits or work shadowing you have undertaken.)
- Please list any academic work you have had published together with the name of the publisher or the journal which has accepted it. (Enclose abstracts or summaries).
- Applicants for taught courses state the reason for wishing to pursue the course for which you have applied. (Show that you are well informed about the course and stress any parts of your first degree – such as a final year project – that are relevant to it.)

Instruction for drama, music, English and MBA applicants:

'Please enclose with your application two examples (non-returnable) of your written work in the English language. These should be academic essays and need not be more than 2,000 words each. For Drama the essays may be reviews of productions.'

Vocational courses

Application forms for these courses contain sections which must be completed very carefully since they are designed to test your suitability for the course. For example, when making an application for a course in social work it is essential to write about any work experience or voluntary work you have done in a social work setting – and to explain what you gained from it; to describe social work settings you have visited and again what you gained from doing so. Similarly, teacher training applicants need to write about school experience. An application for law should contain details of relevant experience – for instance in solicitors' offices or in Chambers and information on any visits you have made to courts – but even some apparently non-relevant experience can be useful. Work experience with a surveyor could well be of interest if you have said elsewhere on the form that you might ultimately want to specialise in property law.

See the profile of Janet Hughes (page 132) for examples of searching questions asked of candidates for a vocational course.

Can I enclose additional information?

Unless specifically instructed not to do so. Application forms do not, in every case, give you enough space to answer all the questions thoroughly. If this is so, there is nothing wrong in enclosing a covering letter giving more detail – as long as you do genuinely need the space. A letter written simply for the sake of writing a letter doesn't help. Rather than showing extra diligence and motivation it merely serves to irritate the person reading it!

Research proposals

If you are applying to do a research degree you will probably be asked to include a short outline of your intended project (research proposal). It is easier to complete this after you have made a few informal visits. If possible, try to make use of input from a potential supervisor. Failing that, you could enlist the assistance of a lecturer in your current department. You may, alternatively, be asked to put this proposal in a separate letter.

The quality of your proposal will influence not only the departmental staff responsible for deciding whether or not to accept you but also any funding body you approach.

Instruction taken from an application form:

'Applicants for a higher degree course by research, leading either to an MPhil or to a PhD, must state the title or area of the proposed research topic on the form, and must enclose a description in about 300 words of the proposed research. If you wish to conduct part of your research elsewhere than at the University, you should indicate this, with details, in your Additional Statement. Indicate with which academic member of staff you would like to work, if known.'

A tip on choosing your academic referee. It need not be your personal tutor if there is someone else in the department who knows your potential for the given area of research better. It is a courtesy to discuss using another person with your tutor however.

Most places will not accept an open testimonial but ask instead for a confidential reference. In order to avoid delay, some institutions ask you to enclose it with the application form. In order to be sure that you have not read it, they will ask for it to be sent in a sealed envelope with the referee's signature written across the seal. (Whether or not your referee does in fact choose to discuss the reference with you is at his or her discretion!)

WHAT WILL HAPPEN AT AN INTERVIEW?

For some courses it probably won't follow the format of one for a job. It may well be quite informal. That doesn't mean that it is a mere formality however. It would still be worth attending any sessions being organised by your careers advisory service on interviews and applications, even though you are not job hunting like some of the other students on your course.

If you are applying for a research programme there will be detailed discussion about your proposed research area and the mutual suitability of yourself and the department. (Can they assist you? Have they got anyone to supervise you? etc.)

Expect the interview to cover:

- Your reasons for wishing to do the course.
- Future plans – for after you have completed it.
- Any relevant experience you have. This could be extra-curricular activities and even voluntary work in the case of a postgraduate diploma or certificate course.

You may be asked some questions designed to see how you would handle a particular problem.

Interviews for vocational courses can take different formats. They may include:

- aptitude and/or personality tests
- group discussions between candidates – designed to test clarity in expressing ideas, listening skills and ability to consider other people's points of view.
- panel interviews
- a series of one-to-one interviews with different members of staff.

You will be expected to ask questions too. It is a good idea to have some ready – and to have written them down. You'll want to know about:

- **Funding** The interviewer may be able to suggest sources you had not thought of.
- **Progression from the course** What have previous students gone on to do? Particularly with regard to conversion courses and vocational certificate and diploma courses, you could ask about the employment rate of former students.
- **Facilities**, particularly library and computer space. Does the department have its own reference material in addition to that in the general library? Can you use computers at any time of day or night? That is particularly important as Ralph Blaney (page 130) discovered: 'The Internet gets busy when America wakes up.'

Offers of places may be made at the interview or later. Many will be conditional on your gaining a specified class of degree.

THE CLEARING HOUSES

Graduate Teacher Training Registry (GTTR)

GTTR is a central agency which acts as a clearing house for applicants to Post Graduate Certificate in Education courses at universities, colleges of higher education and certain groups of schools in England and Wales – for example Bromley Schools Collegiate and City Technology Trusts Smallpiece Programme.

GTTR processes applications on behalf of its member institutions. Organisations outside the GTTR scheme are the Open University, Bolton Institute, University of Surrey and the University of Wales College, Cardiff.

Scottish and Northern Ireland PGCE courses are not in GTTR.

How and when do I make a GTTR application?

In the summer term prior to entry

Telephone or write to the GTTR to request an application pack to be sent to you as soon as they are available – usually early August. It is advisable to contact GTTR earlier than this as requests are kept on a database ready for despatch of information as soon as possible.

From September 1st

1. Contact the GTTR enclosing a registration fee (£6 in 1996). You will receive a *Guide to Applicants* together with an application form.
2. Research and consult prospectuses from each of the institutions in which you are interested.

3. You may select up to four institutions – and you put these on the application form in order of preference.
4. The completed form should by passed to a referee who, in turn, adds a confidential reference and sends the form to GTTR.
5. GTTR send you an acknowledgement card immediately.
6. All details of your application are added to computer records at GTTR.
7. GTTR sends you a letter giving you your application number together with a summary of the application. This should be checked and any corrections notified immediately to GTTR.

Mid October

1. GTTR makes a reduced size copy of your application form which is sent, in turn, to each institution you listed. Forms are despatched one day a week to institutions, normally a Thursday.
2. Referral to 2nd, 3rd or 4th choice is made if you have been unsuccessful in previous choices.
3. GTTR computer records all details of the progress of your application and keeps both you and institutions informed.
4. Institutions endeavour to send an invitation to attend for interview within three weeks of receiving the paperwork from GTTR. Institutions are required to inform GTTR within three weeks of receiving forms what their intention is.
5. Within three weeks of interviews, institutions must let GTTR know the outcome.

Closing Date

GTTR does not have a closing date but applications should be made as soon as possible as courses fill up early. In fact, many primary courses are full by December.

Unsuccessful Applicants

The application form has a section which may be completed by candidates if they wish to identify alternative selections, should they be unsuccessful with their initial choices. In this section, applicants may select by region or simply indicate that they are prepared to consider any institution within the scheme.

Note on PGCE courses in art

A different clearing house, ADAR, used to act as the clearing house for 13 specialist centres offering Art and Design Postgraduate Certificate in Education courses.

ADAR has now merged with GTTR and applications for courses commencing academic year 1997/98 will be dealt with as other PGCE applications.

What about law?

Central Applications Board (Law)

The Central Applications Board co-ordinates most, but not all, full time Common Professional Examination and Postgraduate Diploma in Law courses in England and Wales. The application procedure is this:

1. In the Autumn of their final year, intending students should contact the Board for an application pack.
2. Candidates should complete the application form naming up to nine institutions in order of preference.
3. There is a closing date – usually in mid February – by which time the completed form, together with a registration fee, should be returned to the Central Applications Board.
4. Forms are initially sent to only the first three centres listed on the application form.
5. Details are sent to other centres only if no offers of places are made.
6. Details of offers should have been received by applicants by the end of April.

7. By the end of May applicants must confirm acceptance of one offer. At this stage a deposit (the amount is decided by the named institution) is payable.

- Late places may sometimes be available due to people withdrawing from the scheme, often due to financial difficulties.
- As actual dates vary from year to year, you should check with the Board to find out the time scale and closing dates.
- In recent years, competition for places on the CPE courses has been fierce. An upper second class degree is generally the minimum requirement. Students who have gained legal work experience or can demonstrate a commitment to a career in the legal profession also have an advantage.
- It is worth knowing that selectors for many courses only consider candidates who have placed them in their first three preferences.
- Although the closing date is in February candidates are advised to apply as early as possible.

And social work?

Social Work Admissions System (SWAS) – England and Wales

SWAS is the central admissions system you would use to apply for postgraduate courses in social work, probation work and education social work (formerly known as education welfare work).

Although the closing date for application is mid December – usually around the 15th – applications are dealt with on a first-come, first-served basis, so it pays to get in early. Applications made *before the closing date* have been rejected because courses are already full. In addition to this, you again need to know about funding implications – another reason to start your research early. For example, if you wished to take a course in education social work you would not be eligible for a bursary from the Central Council for Education and Training in Social Work.

The SWAS system works as follows:

1. Applicants obtain the form, ask permission from two referees to give their names and hand the completed form plus fee (currently £8) to one of them. The first referee writes a confidential reference and sends all the paperwork to SWAS. The second referee is asked to send his or her reference to SWAS under separate cover.
2. SWAS sends copies of the form to all the institutions named on it.
3. Applications received after the December closing date but before mid May are classified as 'late' and sent to institutions only if they still have vacancies.
4. When candidates receive an offer of a place the institution accepting them sends an application form on which to apply for a grant (if relevant). These are returned to CCETSW – the address can be found on page 161.

- You must be able to demonstrate a knowledge of and motivation for social work. On the form you are asked to indicate the type of work you want to do and to write a lengthy personal statement.
- Some courses require candidates to present a portfolio, containing details of relevant experience.
- Different references are required from the two referees. One must be a comment on the applicant's suitability for a career in social work; the second, an assurance that the applicant is capable of following an advanced course of study.

CALENDAR

In the year BEFORE your final year

Start research. Decide between taught or research programme. Ask advice. Check sources of funding. Check entry requirements and selection procedure. Would relevant summer vacation work improve your chances? If so, try to arrange some.

If you are hoping to study abroad, check qualifications required and need for any tests, e.g. GMAT (taken in June).

Final Year

September onwards

Apply to PGCE courses.
Apply for Diploma in Social Work courses.
Apply for CPE/Diploma in Law courses.

October – December

Study postgraduate prospectuses.
Make informal visits to different universities and departments.
Find out about sources of funding.
Some courses and scholarships have closing dates now.
Look in the national press and on your careers service noticeboard for details of advertised research posts and studentships.
Make applications.
Mid December is the closing date for SWAS.

January – Easter

Finish making applications.
The Government Research Councils announce their research awards and advise universities (who then advertise them).
Check funding bodies' deadlines and apply.
NB Deadline for CPE courses is in mid February.
Possibly attend interviews.

Easter onwards

Some funding council deadlines.
If unsuccessful so far, approach other departments to see if they have late vacancies.

June

Let the institution that has offered you a place know your degree result.

August/September

Some late places may still be available. *The Times* published a special supplement last September, listing them all.

Applications for courses in other countries should be made well in advance. For example applications to universities in the USA should be made 18 months ahead.

It is also important to make applications for courses in this country as early as you possibly can. Whether a course has an official deadline or not, if it is a popular one it will fill up quickly. Val Butcher of Leeds University Careers Advisory Service says, 'The big message is to apply early. The course may be very popular, therefore hard to enter, and it make take some time for a decision to come through. If a student intends to apply for a Career Development Loan, this can't be finalised until a firm offer of a place has been received. Another advantage is that if you are interviewed early in the year, the rest of the year is free for you to concentrate on academic work.'

ADVICE

Professor Bruce Sellwood works at Reading University in the Post-graduate Research Institute of Sedimentology – where he assesses applications for the MSc/Diploma course in Sedimentology and its Applications. The course has between 15 and 18 students each year with applications averaging 80. This includes United Kingdom, European Union and foreign students. Bruce's students have arrived from Italy, Spain and Algeria. 'Fifteen is the optimum number as the course is very equipment biased with lots of hands on work.'

Although a variety of subjects are acceptable for entry to this MSc, Bruce says that most applicants have earth sciences as a background. A former student whose subject was organic chemistry withdrew due to difficulties adapting to the geological content. But there are students on the course with less apparently relevant first degrees. A current student who Bruce feels is 'going to be good' has a science based archaeology degree from University College, London. His undergraduate dissertation had a geological bias.

Applications start landing on Bruce's desk in October, peaking around February/March – 'with the rest deciding to go for the MSc after finals.' Apart from new graduates, some applicants have had a gap of several years, maybe doing something menial in the oil industry, say on an oil rig, to get the cash to see them through the year. Applicants need to offer a first or upper second class degree. This is, in any case, essential to get any Natural Environment Research Council funding.

What has made students decide to apply to this course? 'Earth science students who are interested in postgraduate courses often get good advice from their tutors. Staff and student numbers are on the small side and there's a good informal network. It's a subject where everyone knows everyone.' (For example, Bruce crosses the border to teach some parts of Heriot-Watt's course and a lecturer from Newcastle heads south to instruct on an aspect of Reading's course.) Bruce welcomes students approaching him for informal advice, but they would then need to complete Reading's 'Application for admission as a postgraduate student' form, and despatch it to the Science Faculty Office.

Interviews are not compulsory due to the high cost of travelling. However, Bruce feels interviews are useful 'so that we can see them and they can see us.' Courses are different. Reading's course is unique as a full time course within sedimentology, although there are a small number of related courses elsewhere. For instance it is possible to tackle petroleum geology and geophysics at Imperial College or micropalaeontology at Southampton. Everyone is offered an extended telephone interview.

Expect to be questioned very closely on your reasons for choosing your research topic or, if you are applying for a taught course, for choosing particular options. Professor John Macklin of Leeds University's Spanish and Portuguese Department says, 'We pay a lot of attention to the research proposal in the case of research applicants and to the chosen options and proposed dissertation topic for those applying for a taught master's. We also ask why they want to come to us – although we know they will have made other applications. We give a lot of weight to their own thinking. References also are of course very important.

11 FUNDING

HOW DO I FINANCE A POSTGRADUATE COURSE?

Like most students on their first degree courses, you probably had your fees paid, and also something towards living expenses.

Unfortunately the picture changes dramatically at postgraduate level. The fortunate few are future teachers where local education authorities are required to give an award. If you are contemplating extending your university days on an MA, MSc, MPhil, PhD, or certificate or diploma, the hunt for cash can be long and complicated and requires careful planning. As well as the fees, a UK student is likely to need between £5,000 and £6,000 a year, but you may spend far more. An overseas student will need more.

Different organisations can offer funding for different courses. Most funding comes from Research Councils and other national award bodies such as the British Academy Humanities Research Board. Some courses, such as the MBA, are not eligible for any government funding. There is competition for available funds and availability varies a lot between subjects. It can be extremely difficult and competitive on the arts and humanities side. In contrast, if you are a scientist or technologist you might stand more chance of finding someone to help.

DOES THE CLASS OF MY DEGREE MAKE ANY DIFFERENCE?

Yes, it is usually an important factor. Research Council funding – and awards from individual departments where they have them – are usually awarded on a competitive basis.

WHO GIVES WHAT?

Research Councils provide funding mainly via:

- advanced course studentships for one year MSc courses
- research studentships for PhDs.

There are also variations in the research studentships which are known as

CASE – Co-operative Awards in Science and Engineering – in collaboration with a commercial or government funded partner. Full details are available in the Research Councils' annual booklets.

Research Councils mainly allocate a quota of awards to university departments. Candidates are then nominated by the department.

All figures are for 1996/97 unless otherwise stated.

The Biotechnology and Biological Sciences Research Council (BBSRC)

Subjects – agriculture and related subjects, biochemistry, biological sciences, food and related subjects, and some engineering.

Types of award

1. Standard research studentship for PhD.
2. Co-operative Award in Science and Engineering (CASE) and 'Industrial' CASE, where a student is jointly supervised by a university and an industrial company.
3. 'Special' studentship for areas of high priority.
4. Veterinary research fellowships for outstanding veterinary students to do research in biological sciences relevant to veterinary medicine.
5. Advanced course / research master's studentship for one year MSc courses.

Academic requirements For research studentships and research master's studentships, a first or upper second. For advanced course studentships, a first or second.

Closing date 31 July.

How much is the award worth? Standard research studentship/one year studentship – £6,700 (London), £5,400 (elsewhere). Special research studentship – £8,530 (London), £6,680 (elsewhere). Plus extra allowances. Fees paid at current BBSRC approved rates.

The Economic and Social Research Council (ESRC)

Subjects – social science subjects. Some subjects are borderline, for instance cultural and media studies. If in doubt check with both the ESRC and the British Academy, before 15 March.

Types of award

1. Standard research studentship for M. Phil and PhD, available on a competitive basis. 363 were awarded in 1995.
2. Collaborative Awards in Science and Engineering research studentship – for projects with companies. Available on a quota basis. 69 were awarded in 1995.
3. Science, Technology and Innovative Studies research studentships (STIS), available on a quota basis.
4. Advanced course studentships for one year master's courses, available on quota and competition basis. 612 were given in 1995.

Academic requirements For all types a first or upper second

Closing date Standard research studentships – 1 May; CASE and STIS – nominations by 1 July; Advanced course studentships – competition students – 1 May, quota nominations, 1 June.

How much is the award worth? All studentships – £6720 (London), £5190 (elsewhere), plus special allowances. Approved fees paid.

The Engineering and Physical Sciences Research Council (EPSRC)

Subjects – engineering, physical science, mathematics and information technology.

Types of award

All quota awards:

1. Research studentships for PhDs.
2. Co-operative Awards in Science and Engineering – for topics specified by industrial co-operating bodies.
3. Advanced course studentships for one year master's courses. Various other schemes, such as the Total Technology Scheme.

Academic requirements For research studentships, at least an upper second. For advanced course studentships, a lower second.

Closing date 31 July.

How much is the award worth? All awards – £6,720 (London), £5,190 (elsewhere) with £350 extra for CASE studentships. Plus allowances and fees.

The Medical Research Council (MRC)

Subjects – biomedical subjects.

Types of award

1. Research studentships for PhDs/DPhils.

2. Collaborative research studentships and industrial collaborative research studentships for PhDs and DPhils in conjunction with a company or public sector laboratory.
3. Advanced course studentships/research master's studentships for one year courses.

Academic requirements For all types of research studentship and research master's, at least an upper second. For advanced course studentships, at least a second class degree.

Closing date 27 September.

How much is the award worth? All types of research studentships: £8,943 (London), £6,731 (elsewhere) with increases in subsequent years, plus special allowances. Approved fees paid. Same rate for one year research master's programme. Advanced course studentships: £8,726 (London), £6,567 (elsewhere), plus special allowances. Approved fees paid.

The Natural Environment Research Council (NERC)

Subjects – earth observation, earth sciences, freshwater sciences, marine and atmospheric sciences and terrestrial sciences.

Types of award

1. Research studentships for PhDs.
2. Research Co-operative Awards in Sciences of the Environment (CASE) studentships, where a student is jointly supervised by a university and an external organisation. Also Industrial CASE.
3. Advanced course studentships for one year MSc courses and research master's training awards for an MRes qualification.

Academic requirements For research studentships and research masters, a first or upper second. For advanced course studentships, a first or second.

Closing date 15 August

How much is the award worth? £6,700 (London), £5,400 (elsewhere), with £350 extra for CASE studentships. Plus allowances for dependants, disabled students etc. Approved fees paid.

The Particle Physics and Astronomy Research Council (PPARC)

Subjects – particle physics, astronomy and astrophysics, solar system science.

Please see the entry for EPSRC as PPARC studentships are subject to their rules.

RESEARCH COUNCIL BUDGETS IN 1995/96

BBSRC	£161.6 million
EPSRC	£365.7 million
ESRC	£61.2 million
MRC	£277.8 million
NERC	£155.4 million
PPARC	£196.4 million.

Ministry of Agriculture, Fisheries and Food (MAFF)

Subjects – agriculture, agricultural science, horticulture, rural estate management, agricultural economics, engineering and business aspects of agriculture.

Types of awards

1. Research studentships
2. Advanced course studentships, normally for one year courses, but exceptionally for a two year course.

Academic requirements For research studentships, an upper second. For advanced course studentships in agricultural science, a lower second, but in all other subjects, a lower OR upper second.

Closing date 31 July.

How much is the award worth? All types: £7,072 (London), £5,638 (elsewhere). Plus allowances. Approved fees paid.

British Academy – Humanities Research Board

Subjects – archaeology, classics, drama and theatre studies, English, film studies, history, history of art and architecture, law, linguistics, modern languages, music, philosophy and theology. Some aspects of these subjects are excluded, usually in the social sciences.

Types of award

1. Competition A – studentships for master's or similar courses, lasting between one and two years. Also a programme of research lasting one year.
2. Competition B – for a three year research programme leading to a PhD.
3. Partnership awards with institutions for research already taking place in an institution.

Academic requirements For all awards – a first or upper second.

Closing date 1 May (through the institution where you intend to study).

How much is the award worth?

1. Competitions A and B – £6,720 (London), £5,190 (elsewhere), plus special allowances. Approved fees paid.
2. Partnership awards – half the cost of tuition and fees and half the maintenance grant.

As has already been mentioned, competition for awards in humanities is intense. Information provided in 1996 states that in Competition B, 'Last Year 442 out of 472 awards went to students who had already undertaken postgraduate study; only 6% of undergraduate applicants in Competition B were successful. Furthermore, last year over 1,000 of the applicants in Competition A had a first class degree, but only 500 awards were available.'

NB If you are an international student, coming from one of the EEA countries, you can apply for fees-only awards from UK Government funding bodies.

The Central Council for Education and Training in Social Work (CCETSW)

Subjects:

1. Postgraduate DipSW courses.
2. Post Qualifying Study Programmes.
3. Non graduate DipSW courses where applicants have a first degree.

Types of award

Bursary scheme. CCETSW allocates a quota of bursaries to each course, in proportion to the number of places available. They are means tested.

How much is the award worth? Basic maintenance bursary: £3,381 (London), £2,656 (elsewhere). Additional payments for extra weeks.

Department for Employment and Education (DfEE)

Subjects – library and information science, art and design, drama, language interpretation, film and TV studies and other similar courses.

Types of award

1. Bursaries for full time professional or vocational courses, in the above subjects.
2. Advanced course studentships for master's degrees in librarianship or MScs in Information Science.
3. Research studentships for research in librarianship or information science for an MPhil or PhD. These are means tested.

Academic requirements For advanced course studentships, a first or second. For research studentships, a first or upper second.

Closing date Bursaries – 1 June. Advanced course studentships in librarianship – 31 May; information science – 1 August. Research studentships – 1 May. Institutions submit the forms.

How much is the award worth? Bursaries: £3,460 (London), £2,735 (elsewhere). Additional payments for extra weeks and other allowances. Approved fees. Studentships: £5,845 (London), £4,645 (elsewhere), plus other allowances and approved fees.
Please note that as of April 1997 enquiries regarding DfEE Bursaries and studentships should be directed to the British Academy. (See contact details on page 161.)

Local Education Authorities (LEAs)

Mandatory means tested awards are available for postgraduate certificate in education courses (PGCE). The rates in 96/97 were £2,105 (London), £1,710 (elsewhere), plus other allowances and approved fees. Bursaries have been available for shortage subjects. These are now being replaced by the 'Priority Subject Recruitment Scheme.' Universities will be expected to bid for funds. The scheme will operate for religious education, IT, modern languages, sciences, mathematics and design technology. At present there are no figures available on the payments under this scheme.

Is the PGCE the only award that LEAs give?

LEAs can also make discretionary awards for courses that do not come under the remit of other award making bodies. There is, however, a great deal of variation between authorities and there is no standard grant.

- Some authorities offer no support for postgraduate study, whilst others consider only certain courses.
- You need to contact your own authority early in the year as closing dates are usually around March to June. In some cases applications are dealt with on a first-come, first-served basis.
- Prospects of getting help are improved if the course is vocational and is a specific requirement for a career.
- You also need to present a good case for receiving the award.

Regional award making organisations

If you come from Scotland, Northern Ireland, the Isle of Man, and the Channel Islands you may be eligible for funding from one of the following organisations. (See page 159 for contact details.)

Student Awards Agency for Scotland

Department of Education for Northern Ireland

States of Jersey, Education Department

States of Guernsey, States Education Council

Isle of Man, Department of Education

You need to know that:

- All award making organisations have eligibility rules. These relate to residency in the United Kingdom, with special rules for refugees and migrant workers. In many instances there are fees only awards for candidates from the European Union.
- Age limits are variable. For instance, the British Academy has no age limit, whereas the DfEE states that in order to apply for a bursary you must be under 40.

- Additional allowances payable with many awards include: extra money for dependants, disabled students, older students, and field work expenses.

SUMMARY

Where funding is concerned:

- Some subjects are borderline, so it is important to be clear about which organisation to approach.
- On a course there may be some places with funding but also places that do not receive any help.
- It's important to get up to date information about procedures and to stick to closing dates.
- In many cases, as with the Research Councils, the university or college where you want to undertake your postgraduate study submits your application for funding.

ALTERNATIVE SOURCES OF FUNDING

Educational trusts and charities

These organisations can provide help with fees, living expenses and other costs. There are a large number of these bodies but you need to bear in mind that many people apply to them. Realistically, you need to consider the following points, if you want to use this source of funding.

- Trusts expect you to have tried the mainstream sources of funding, and may ask for evidence of this.
- Some offer help only to specific groups, such as those from a particular geographic area or applying for certain courses.
- Money is most likely to be available to students with the greatest needs.

● It is unlikely that money from these sources will go anywhere near meeting the full costs of study.

Contact the Educational Grants Advisory Service for advice.

European social fund

Funding can be obtained from this source for some vocational courses. However there is no central list and money is allocated on an annual basis. You need to find out the current position with course staff. It is not possible to make a direct application.

Research assistantships

As a research assistant you would have the opportunity to do paid work as part of a research team, and carry out work towards a higher degree at the same time.

● Opportunities occur mostly in the pure and applied sciences, and are limited in humanities, arts and social sciences.
● You would need to make sure that the post was geared to a first degree applicant and would allow adequate time for you to complete your PhD.

Teaching Company Scheme (TCS)

This scheme enables you to take part in two year industrial projects, be paid a realistic salary and register for a higher degree. A first degree is required in science, engineering, or business/management. For further information write to TCD, 79 London St, Faringdon, Oxon SN7 8AA.

Training and Enterprise Councils and Local Enterprise Councils

TECs and LECs may be able to help, but there is much regional variation and you will need to approach your own TEC/LEC. At the time of writing Thames Valley TEC and Kent TEC are unable to help with postgraduate courses. However, Merseyside TEC are at present offering some funding for some MSc courses at Liverpool John Moores University. Examples are industrial biotechnology and public administration. This is however, reviewed annually.

An additional difficulty in obtaining funding from these sources is that TECs and LECs are geared to local labour market needs. If there is no perceived need for people with particular qualifications in their area they are not likely to agree to funding requests.

University scholarships

Scholarships are often offered by universities. In most cases they are for a particular subject or course, but some give other kinds. For example, Bath, Birmingham, Cardiff, Glamorgan, Loughborough and Stirling offer sports bursaries to outstanding athletes and players. Details of scholarships and bursaries are available in university calendars or directly from departments. The Open University also has some limited funding of its own to assist some students who cannot get assistance from other sources.

Other scholarships

These may come from various sources like learned bodies and institutions. One example is the Institute of Historical Research which awards nine fellowships each year to cover the final year of a PhD, and several smaller scholarships of £500 maximum to enable non-supported research students to undertake research overseas or to attend short skills courses.

Loans

If, like many postgraduates, you have to face up to paying your own way, one of the first sources to know about is the Career Development Loan scheme (CDL).

This scheme is available through a partnership arrangement between the Department for Education and Employment and four banks – Barclays, the Co-operative, Clydesdale and the Royal Bank of Scotland. It can be used to finance courses that are vocational and last up to two years.

- You can borrow from £200 to £8,000 to pay up to 80% of the fees and other expenses, for example for books and equipment. (Applicants who have been out of work for three months at the time of application can apply for a loan to cover 100% of the course fees if the application is endorsed by their TEC or LEC.)
- During the course, and for up to one month afterwards, the interest is paid for you. After that, you must start the repayments and pay interest on terms agreed with the bank.
- Depending on your circumstances, repayments can be deferred for a further five months.

Over 13,000 people took out loans in 1995/1996. (Not all were postgraduate students however.)

Other loans

- Postgraduate Certificate in Education courses qualify for student loans.
- For other courses, it may be possible to arrange a loan from a bank. The Midland for instance, makes Postgraduate Studies Loans of up to £5,000 per year plus course fees (maximum, two years). There are special terms for legal students.

State benefits

Many courses are available on a part time basis. Under the '21 hour rule' you may be able to study part time and claim benefit, provided that you are willing to give up your course if you are offered a job. Contact your local Benefits Agency branch for more details.

Employers

Assistance is sometimes available from commercial or industrial companies, and professional bodies. However, some of them may expect you to work for them for a year or so, before approaching them for help.

Some examples:

- Currently the Association of British Insurers is offering three scholarships for postgraduate study for research degrees. Exceptional applicants who want to take a taught postgraduate degree will also be considered. The research must have some relevance to insurance.
- Law bursaries are available from the Windsor Fellowship, in association with some companies, for ethnic minority students entering the LPC or Bar Vocational course.
- It is possible to get assistance from large firms of solicitors who sponsor trainee solicitors through the LPC and /or CPE course.
- Students are often sponsored through postgraduate courses in actuarial science.
- Economists are sometimes sponsored through master's courses by the Bank of England.

Work

Can you realistically hold down part time work while on a full time course?

This will depend partly on the course and partly on your own time management skills and energy. Because postgraduate students work much longer hours than undergraduates, it will not be as easy to work for several hours a week in the local pub, pizza house etc. as it was as an undergraduate. (It is now estimated that most undergraduates work for at least 12 hours per week in term time in addition to any full time vacation work they can find.)

You will find that not only are you required to put in more weekly hours in order to cope with the course, but that the precious Easter and summer vacations are swallowed up in project work. However, where there's a will there's a way – and you might be able to fit in some part time employment. There are other possibilities (for the fortunate few).

Some students earn money from demonstrating to undergraduates. This has the advantage of being done in the department where you are registered (no time consuming travelling or expenditure on fares).

Others, if their research is in a relevant field such as IT or computing, may be able to supplement their incomes considerably through consultancy work. Stephanie Fountain, who is doing a PhD in Computer Vision (see page 135), is doing exactly that.

New ruling

Under new rules announced by the Inland Revenue in May 1996, students over the age of 30 who are in *full time* attendance on courses lasting 12 months may claim tax relief on their tuition fees. This may help some students who are seriously having to consider financing themselves.

Professor Bruce Sellwood of Reading University advises that all prospective postgraduate students need to think carefully about acquiring the cash to fund their course. 'Reading have three Advanced Course Studentships from the Natural Environmental Research Council. These are divided in to half units so that a student gets half the fees and half the full award for living expenses. The rate for maintenance for 1996/1997 is £5,400 for universities outside London. There is no magic solution to finding the rest of the money. Most students have saved while working, are helped by their families or organise a Career Development Loan for themselves.' Studentships from NERC are under review and Bruce feels that the 'help is likely to go down next year.' Encouragingly though, no one has dropped out for financial reasons. However, the occasional foreign student has had difficulties in the past. Students also have to find the cash for two days field work in East Anglia and Yorkshire. This comes to around £220. Another extra is the cost of the field work for the dissertation.

CHECKLIST OF QUESTIONS TO ASK

- What scholarships and bursaries are available?
- From which sources?
- Am I aware of all the relevant closing dates?
- Could I earn any money through teaching/demonstrating? What are the rates of pay?

All the information in this chapter was correct at the time of writing but is subject to change. It is very important to obtain the latest information.

12 LIFE AS A POSTGRADUATE

WHAT WILL IT BE LIKE? WILL IT BE VERY DIFFERENT FROM LIFE AS A FIRST DEGREE STUDENT?

Yes, it will certainly be different. For a start there may be fewer students on your particular course. In some departments you could be one of only a handful of students. You will, in most cases, even on a taught course, be expected to work much more on your own. Remember the feeling three or four years ago when you had to make the adjustment from school to the demands of university study? The transition probably won't be as great as that however. You are also likely to be mixing with a wider range of students from different backgrounds.

The postgraduate year is 44 weeks, but in these weeks you will also be working much longer hours – certainly as a research student. Professor Michael Lea of Royal Holloway says, 'It becomes much more like being at work. Students put in very long days – and you won't find many postgrads taking the entire Easter vacation as holiday for instance. But in many projects students can be very flexible as to when they work, and this can be an attraction.'

What about working methods?

There will be a major difference according to whether you are taking a taught or research-based course. On the first, you will have intensive days, filled with what is called 'contact time' – lectures, seminars, classes and so on – and will have to work on your projects in the evenings and at weekends. On the second, you will have to work just as hard but there will be no timetable, other than at the beginning if your course includes tuition in skills training. The person who fixes your timetable will be – yourself! You may even be responsible for deciding how frequently and when to see your supervisor.

Who else will be on the course?

Some students will be new graduates. Others may have been at work for several years. Yet others may be mature students who are returning to university after a considerable time gap. Some are likely to be from overseas. The positive side of all this is that it can be very enriching experience. Ralph Blaney, who is doing a PhD at Reading University (see page 130), says that being in the minority both age and nationality wise – most of the students are in their thirties and forties and from other countries – has meant that he gets to learn about different places without leaving the UK.

Aren't postgraduates isolated?

They were regarded as such once certainly. Midway between undergraduates and academic staff they may have led a rather lonely existence – at some places. At some they may still do so. Research students in the humanities may find research in libraries and archives somewhat lonely. Meeting other postgraduate students socially can make all the difference. Sharing accommodation could be one way. There are universities that have separate wings in halls of residence for postgraduate students, which means that a group of students has a natural meeting place.

How will I meet other students?

Again, think back to your first days as an undergraduate. How did you meet people then? Through lectures? By being in a hall of residence? By joining student societies? All these avenues are still open. If you are on a course with small numbers, the lecture route may be the least positive but the other methods are still there. Even though there is no equivalent of the Freshers' Fair, with keen societies after your subscription, there is usually nothing to stop postgraduates joining any society that interests them. Also, many universities have postgraduate societies. Given the larger number of postgraduates in general, the likelihood of being able to meet people from different course but with similar interests has increased. BUT – you will have to start early. One thing most postgraduate students mention is how quickly the time flies. A year – which is not a year at all but from September/October until June – flies past. You can't think, 'Six weeks gone already. Never mind I'm here for three years. Plenty of time to meet people.'

Graduate schools

Thirty five universities and colleges now have these. They may be a single unit accommodating all postgraduates at an institution as at the University of Warwick, where there are over 5,000 postgraduate students (40% of the student population), or a faculty based school as at Bradford, where a graduate school for the Social Science Faculty has recently opened.

Graduate schools offer the following advantages:

- They make interdisciplinary research easier.
- They enable postgraduates to meet each other.
- They assist staff student relations.
- They provide dedicated facilities like computers solely for research students – which are available during the undergraduate vacations.

Where will I live?

Any of:

- postgraduate hall of residence
- postgraduate annexe to a hall of residence
- ordinary hall of residence
- institution owned flat or house
- private accommodation.

NB It should be easier to find a house or flat to rent once you are a postgraduate. Most landlords regard them more favourably than undergraduates.

What will the course cost? How much must I expect to budget for?

This is an all-important question, particularly so if you have ploughed your way through Chapter 11 on funding – or the lack of it.

It is generally accepted now that undergraduates need at least £4,000 a year to meet term time expenditure. Unfortunately your costs are going to be higher, because you will need to devote most of the vacation to academic work also. You will probably, and almost certainly, if you are a research student, be going to spend most of the year in residence.

Tuition fees were something you didn't need to worry about as an undergraduate. Now you do. If you can find an organisation to take care of these, that is one headache less. If not, your annual expenditure could run to £10,000. Tuition fees average at £2,500 but vary from £1,600 to over £4,000.

Then there are ordinary living expenses. The weekly amount need not be very different from what you needed as an undergraduate, except that you might need to spend more on books and equipment. Surveys last year showed that most postgraduate students were spending £200–400 on these items. Other costs will obviously vary according to where you are living and what your personal tastes are. Hall fees increase by an average of 5–8% a year, so look in prospectuses to see what these are and add the additional amount. They vary from institution to institution. They can be as little as £30 a week (in certain towns) for self catering and well over £70 if most meals are included. Renting in the private sector, as you are almost certainly aware, could cost from £40 per week upwards – with the emphasis on the 'upwards'. People spend differing amounts on food, depending on whether or not they are fully self catering. Say, £1,100 a year?

Then items like laundry, clothes, entertainment and miscellaneous expenditure could run away with a further £500–£600. In all, you will probably need £5,000–£6,000 in addition to fees.

CHECKLIST OF QUESTIONS TO ASK

- What is social life like for postgraduates?
- Is there a postgraduate society and what events does it organise?
- Is there a postgraduate common room within the department – or a room for use jointly by postgraduates and staff?
- How much does accommodation cost?
- Are postgraduates given assistance in finding any?
- Are there hall places for postgraduates?
- Could I bring my family?

Additional questions for research students

- What personal facilities will I be provided with? i.e. desk, filing cabinet, telephone. You can expect to share a room – usually with other postgraduates – but there are horror stories of postgrads at some places being expected to share a desk.
- Where is the nearest photocopier? (Quite important.) And do I have to pay to take copies? (It should be included in the fees you pay!)

Lee West, who is a PhD student at Birmingham University says, 'In my opinion the major difference between being a postgraduate and an undergraduate is the way in which you learn. When you are an undergraduate you know what to learn by your lecture courses. However, when you are a postgrad you have to essentially teach yourself what you need to learn. By this, I don't just mean topics from books but also tools necessary to do your work. In my case that meant quite a few different computer packages. Also you have to specialise in the area you are working in.

'Another difference is that when you are a postgraduate it is almost like having a nine to five job (even though you may work from 11 to 7). This quite different from being an undergraduate and having three to four lectures a day on average. It takes a bit of getting used to.

'A PhD is definitely not like a third year project as it takes one of the years to get familiar with the research topic. It is definitely challenging and demanding – especially the writing up – but very rewarding.

'In doing my PhD I have learned how to give talks and to write scientific documents as well as the research material. I have also travelled quite a bit, as for twelve months I was stationed out at an experiment in Geneva. This was one of the perks of doing high energy physics.'

TIPS

- Postgraduate courses are intensive. In order to cope, work regular hours each day as though you were in a paid job.
- Set yourself reasonable targets.
- Socialise. Do not become isolated.
- Set a financial budget for your expenses and stick to it.

Research students in particular:

- Keep to a disciplined work programme.
- Keep a diary of development and progress.
- Discuss chapters of your thesis with your supervisor as you write them.
- Try to find paid tutorial or demonstrating work by looking on noticeboards, word of mouth etc.
- Enquire about becoming an assistant warden of a hall of residence and living rent free.
- Know when to take a break!

HEALTH WARNING

It is all too easy when a deadline approaches to spend long hours hunched in front of a word processor. It is known that keyboard operators have an increased risk of tension neck syndrome. Employers have to obey regulations respecting the use of VDUs. You are your own boss – but when you are rushing to complete a thesis, the last thing you are likely to worry about is your work environment. You may well be given some guidelines. One institution is even now planning some, after two of its lecturers gave themselves muscle strain while completing their own PhD theses. If not, here are some.

- Beware RSI – repetitive strain injury.
- Change your position as often as possible.
- Don't overstretch your fingers.
- Take frequent breaks.
- Intersperse word processing time with other tasks.
- Make sure you sit in a properly (ergonomically) designed chair which can be adjusted to your height.
- To avoid eye strain don't face a window or source of bright light – and keep your screen clean.

THE NATIONAL POSTGRADUATE COMMITTEE (NPC)

This is an all-important organisation.

Why?

Because it is the only organisation that represents the interests of postgraduates specifically. It:

- is made up of student representatives from institutions with postgraduate students
- aims to promote their interests while remaining politically non-aligned
- seeks to influence policy nationally, acting as a campaigning voice and a resource of information for postgraduates
- has links with the NUS, the UK Council for Graduate Education, Research Councils, Government Departments and the media.

Much of the Committee's work lies in giving advice on postgraduate issues and providing means for postgraduates to debate matters of common interest. (Among other things, it organises an annual conference.) Most of its officers are graduates although one full time sabbatical officer is employed.

Among the Committees current concerns are the facts that:

- Some institutions see postgraduate students as a lucrative source of income but have not expanded their facilities sufficiently to cater for them properly or in some cases have designed taught courses very poorly, patching together modules from undergraduate programmes. (This concern is shared by the Harris Committee.)
- Some supervision is less than adequate.

To address these and other issues it has drawn up a Code of Practice which may be obtained from the NPC.

The NPC has produced some booklets which you might like to consult. They should all be available at your present university or college. If you are not a student at present, try the nearest higher education institution (Students' Union, library or careers office), or contact the NPC direct. The booklets are:

- *Guidelines on Codes of Practice for Postgraduate Research*
- *Guidelines for Instructional Postgraduate Courses*
- *Guidelines for the Employment of Postgraduate Students* (covers questions of training, workloads and pay for postgraduates who are given teaching work by their departments)
- *Guidelines for the Conduct of Research Appeals*
- *Guidelines on Accommodation and Facilities for Postgraduate Research* (provision of offices, libraries, computers, common rooms etc.)

Plus

- *The Postgraduate Book* for students' unions to help them provide a better service to postgraduates.

13 ADDITIONAL INFORMATION FOR INTERNATIONAL STUDENTS

International students are very welcome in British universities and if you are thinking about coming here for your postgraduate education all the other chapters in this book are relevant to you. This one addresses some issues which are of relevance only to students from other countries.

Like all other countries Britain has immigration and residence restrictions, designed to prevent non students from coming here under false pretences. So, just as British students planning to study abroad need to check visa and other regulations, you would need to do so well in advance.

WHAT ARE THE IMMIGRATION REQUIREMENTS?

That will depend on your nationality. If you come from an EU country you merely have to get a residence permit – a formality. If you come from elsewhere you may need a visa or entry certificate. A British Council office or the British Embassy or High Commission will be able to advise you.

When you enter Britain the immigration officer at the port or airport will stamp your passport to show whether you need to register with the police. This usually happens if students are not from the EU or from commonwealth countries. Registering isn't difficult. In many cases police officers visit universities and colleges at the beginning of the academic year with all the necessary forms – so students can register there.

Immigration officers will want to know two things:

- Have you sufficient money to cover all your fees and expenses?
- Are you already enrolled on a course which takes more than 15 hours a week? (This is the official definition of a full time student.)

Do I need to get a visa before I come?

Not if you are from the EU or the European Economic Area. Nationals of certain countries do require visas. (The British Embassy or High Commission in your own country will tell you whether this is the case.) If so, you must obtain one before you leave home. If you are not required to obtain a visa, you may wish to obtain something known as 'entry clearance'. This can be done in your home country and will cut down on entry formalities when you arrive here.

HOW GOOD MUST MY ENGLISH BE?

If English is not your first language you will find that most institutions will want evidence of a level of proficiency that means you can benefit from the course you are planning to take. Several different English language test certificates are accepted. The most common ones are:

- the British Council's International English Language Testing System (IELTS) with a score of 6.5 or 7.0 depending on the course you are applying for.
- GCSE/O level English at grade C or above
- A score of 550–600 (again depending on your proposed course) in the TOEFL – which must include a satisfactory mark in the Test of Written English.

COST – IS IT EXPENSIVE TO STUDY IN BRITAIN?

How much will tuition fees be? And what about other living expenses?

See chapter 12 – but remember that you will possibly have additional requirements: for living away from home throughout the whole year and perhaps to fund some travel to other nearby countries.

NB At first you might think that a British postgraduate course looks expensive – but taught courses are usually shorter than in many other countries. That means a saving on tuition fees and general living expenses. Medical care too is free to full-time students on courses which last for more than six months – definitely not the case in many countries.

SOMEWHERE TO LIVE

Will I automatically be allocated accommodation?

No, although many universities and colleges give priority to international students. If they do not allocate you any or if you prefer to live in private accommodation, they will assist you in finding somewhere.

LIFE IN GENERAL

Although I am interested in British culture I want to respect some of my own traditions too. Will this be possible?

Yes. Universities and colleges respect these and in particular help international students to observe religious and dietary requirements. Halls of residence provide a variety of meals. Most universities and colleges have prayer rooms set aside for the use of students of particular faiths.

What help will be given to me in settling in?

That varies from institution to institution, but you might like to consider a university or college that has a large number of international students. There will almost certainly be an International Students' Adviser who will correspond with you before you come, giving you information about the accommodation that has been reserved for you and explaining exactly how to get to the university or college from the airport. After you have arrived, they will:

- introduce you to the university/college and its facilities – often through a pre-term conference, incorporating talks from the different advisers and presentations from student societies
- help you to meet British students – and those of other nationalities
- help you to meet other British people – if you would like to do so
- give you information on possibilities for vacation travel around Britain and the rest of Europe
- act as the first port of call should you have any questions. If students have particular problems, they will refer them to an appropriate person who can help.

CHECKLIST OF QUESTIONS TO ASK

- What are the English language requirements?
- Is there an international students' counsellor?
- Is there an induction period/welcome week?
- What about accommodation?
- Could I bring my family?

(And all the questions in Chapter 12).

ADDITIONAL POINTS

There are over 30,000 students from other countries studying for postgraduate qualifications in Britain.

International students are sometimes eligible to compete for funding from the UK Research Councils.

There are some scholarships and funding schemes available to students from certain countries, from the British Government and from international organisations.

This chapter could continue at length! There are entire books written specially for international students. Among them is one by Trotman and Company – *British University and College Courses*.

14 OPPORTUNITIES OVERSEAS

I WOULD LIKE TO DO MY POSTGRADUATE STUDY IN ANOTHER COUNTRY. HOW DO I SET ABOUT IT?

The first thing to do is start the necessary research about courses very far in advance. Closing dates for applications, timing of courses, even term and semester dates are not always the same as they are here. You will need access to relevant handbooks and prospectuses. Try your careers advisory service as the first point of call. Embassies and high commissions should also be able to help.

WILL MY BRITISH QUALIFICATIONS BE ACCEPTED?

Usually, but not always with ease. This can come as a shock since we pride ourselves on the excellence of our education system. But in some countries degree courses are much more specialised and /or much longer. In many EU countries for example, the idea that anyone could graduate from a first degree course in three years is greeted with incredulity. This is because in other EU countries higher education follows a different pattern from that customary in the UK, Ireland, the USA and Commonwealth countries.

In continental European universities students complete a 'first cycle' – after which very few leave to look for employment – and a 'second cycle'. To complete both cycles takes from four to five years, depending on the country, and it is after the second cycle that students may proceed to doctoral study. On the face of it, it looks as though our bachelor's degrees are gained in a very short time. On the other hand, length does not mean higher quality. UK students often have more specialised entry qualifications when they start their first degree – and this is why our programmes are shorter. It becomes impossible to equate all degrees directly! But certainly Germany and the Netherlands, at least, regard their degrees as equivalent to UK and Irish master's).

None of this means that study in continental Europe is impossible! But getting qualifications recognised and getting a place can be very time consuming!

- Detailed transcripts of your degree programme may be required in order for the institution you wish to attend to be able to make a direct comparison with its own qualifications.
- The possibility of going straight on to a research degree in a EU country without first taking a master's at home OR first completing part of the host country's second cycle is less likely than it is here.

In the USA – in complete contrast – a UK honours degree is sometimes, but not always, rated equally with a US master's degree! Much depends on the American institution awarding the degrees.

So, you need to compare apparently comparable qualifications carefully. It may be that your degree is automatically accepted: it may be that all you need to provide is a detailed transcript of your course. In some countries all applicants to postgraduate courses have to take an entrance test and the mark gained is important.

The reverse of all this holds equally true. You will want to know that the course you are thinking of taking will be accepted over here.

A good source of information is the International Guide to Qualifications in Education, published by UK NARIC (care of the British Council). It compares and evaluates all the qualifications awarded in

150 countries in addition to describing each one's education system. It is not updated every year though, so you will have to double check the information.

Having digested all this, you will be glad to know that there are post-graduate courses in most countries and that, provided you can overcome some common obstacles, there is no reason why you should not study abroad. Courses at business schools in the United States are particularly popular.

You should be able to find prospectuses from universities of several countries in the reference section of your careers advisory service. Some of these are from Commonwealth countries and North America, where there is no language problem. Others are from countries in Europe where the language of instruction is English. Where it is not, there are opportunities to take intensive language and culture courses before enrolling on a postgraduate course proper.

OBSTACLES?

Yes, after the thorny problem of equating qualifications, the most common are:

● Finance.
● Knowledge of another language.

Institutions will require proof of ability in their language and may require English speakers to take a test – just as this is also required by UK institutions of non-native English speakers coming here. Your knowledge of the host country's language would have to be adequate for you to take part fully in seminars as well as produce your written work.

What about cost?

A course taken overseas is almost certainly bound to cost more than to do it here. There are some scholarships available but most students have to fund themselves, as they do here.

There are some specific sources of funding for study in Commonwealth countries: bursaries, grants and loans – some for different forms of postgraduate study, others for postdoctoral research and teaching only. The best source of information on these is in *Awards For Postgraduate Study At Commonwealth Universities*, by the Association of Commonwealth Universities.

EUROPEAN INSTITUTIONS

Two institutions that may be of particular interest to Europhiles are:

The European University Institute, Florence

The Institute, which is jointly funded by member states of the EU, aims to 'contribute to the development of the cultural and scientific heritage of Europe in its unity and variety through activities in the fields of university teaching and research.' It runs three year doctorate programmes and one year master's. Students study in one of four departments: Economics, Law, History and Cultural History and Political and Social Sciences.

Doctoral students produce a thesis – each supervisor has a deliberately small number of students – and must also attend two types of weekly seminar: project seminars for discussing progress and departmental seminars at which all members of a department exchange views and update one another on research programmes.

Research students may complete their entire thesis at the Institute or may be admitted for one or two years to complete a thesis begun at their home university.

- Lecturers are drawn from different countries. The current principal is Irish.
- Interviews are held in March and students are informed of decisions in April. Term starts on 30 August.

- Candidates must have a thorough knowledge of two of the Institute's languages – but the majority of seminars are held in English and French.
- The interview includes a language test.
- Applicants should have at least an upper second and preferably a master's.
- The Institute has an accommodation office.

For the first two years of the course students receive grants from their home governments. (The amount awarded by the British Government for the year 1995/1996 was 560,000 lire per month.) In the third year grants come directly from the Institute. Grants are means tested and are intended to support the student only. There are no additional allowances for dependants. Certain additional sums for travel and health insurance may be claimed.

Students should obtain application forms direct from the Institute. Applications are considered initially by a national selection committee, then by an admissions board consisting of the principal and members of different departments.

Twenty twelve-month Jean Monnet Fellowships for postdoctoral study are awarded annually and advertised every autumn.

The College of Europe

The college is a Postgraduate Institute of European Studies which has as its aim to 'train professionals with European qualifications and experience'. It was originally established at a site in Bruges, but now has a second campus at Natolin just outside Warsaw. It is an independent institution governed by a council which has members from the European Commission and from all EU countries which give it financial support.

Students take a Master of European Studies course, and all must prepare a paper under supervision. Although they enrol to study in

one of four areas – economics, human resources development, law or
political science – there are also compulsory courses in European,
general and interdisciplinary studies.

- Annual intake is 300 students.
- Teaching is done in English and French (plus German at Natolin).
- Students live in halls of residence designed to be like Oxbridge colleges.
- The average age of students is 25.
- Most of them speak four languages!

Most students receive scholarships from their own governments,
although some places are reserved for self funded students. (Fees are
400,000 Belgian francs, which includes accommodation and meals.)

Application forms can be obtained from the UK Committee for the
College of Europe in London, and must be returned by March 15
each year.

COULD I STUDY IN EUROPE FOR PART OF MY POSTGRADUATE COURSE?

The European Commission sponsors a scheme for students to do
exactly this.

ERASMUS

This is part of the wider SOCRATES programme and is therefore
properly know as SOCRATES-ERASMUS, a programme under
which students register at an institution in their own country but
spend part of their course studying in another. No tuition fees are
charged by the institution in the second country – and arrangements
are made through the parent institution. Language tuition is provided where necessary. ERASMUS students receive a small top up
grant to help with additional costs. The programme is best known at
undergraduate level, but students at master's level also participate.

15 STUDENT PROFILES

1. STEPHEN FAYERS, MSc IN SEDIMENTOLOGY AND ITS APPLICATIONS

Having graduated from Portsmouth University in 1994 with a 2.1 in geology, Stephen is now on the MSc in Sedimentology and its Applications in the Postgraduate Research Institute for Sedimentology at Reading University, where he started in October 95. His interest in geology began as a child and he was one of the few to take geology A level. Career planning didn't feature in his final year at Portsmouth as he was busy with the course. So in summer 1994 he was 'looking around here there and everywhere for work.' He was caught in a 'Catch 22' situation. 'For geology-related jobs, you needed experience, but you needed the job to get experience.' At one point he applied for a job with the British Geological Survey, which involved geological mapping in the UK and overseas. He was in competition with 1,300 applicants who were mainly well-qualified graduates and postgraduates!

Volunteer work was the answer for someone needing experience. 'I worked for a year for the British Trust for Conservation Volunteers and Colchester Borough Council. I was based in Chelmsford as a volunteer officer, running working weekends.' The work for the borough council involved conservation and countryside management. Stephen feels that for those intent upon conservation work, doing volunteer work is the best way in.

As the year drew to an end Stephen had to think about his next step. He says, 'I wanted to get back into my subject, so started looking at further study – initially PhDs. My former tutor from Portsmouth suggested MSc courses. During my final year at Portsmouth, the Geological Society had held a milk round in London where I had met the Reading rep. So Reading was on my list along with Portsmouth, Bournemouth, Imperial, University College London and

Royal Holloway College.' The coastal zone management courses at Bournemouth and Portsmouth seemed right for him, but there was no funding.

Stephen feels that major employers like students from well established universities – 'but you need to go and look at departments and make up your own mind. Reading looked the most interesting, so I completed the application form and went for an interview. This was informal. I discussed my voluntary work and undergraduate dissertation on Portland limestone.' An informal offer was made on the spot, with Reading agreeing to recommend Stephen for funding. He says, 'This was a big point for me. It would amount to half the total grant available for maintenance and fees.' In May, he heard that he would get £2,000 for maintenance and that half the cost of his tuition fee would be paid. A further £645 would be paid later for field work. The remainder of his tuition fees came from a Career Development Loan. Stephen says that they are easy to set up up, 'but you really need to read between the lines. The good news is that you pay no interest while on the course, but start paying it back between one and three months after leaving university.' There was a choice between Barclays, the Co-op and the Clydesdale banks, with Barclays being cheaper at the time, at 16.7% interest. Some of Stephen's fellow students have funded the entire course with a Career Development Loan. Others are using savings, or getting family support. A few overseas students are paid by their employers.

The course is hectic, with 15–24 hours taught time each week plus lab and practical work. Stephen says it is a very intensive course crammed into eight months. He feels he covered some of the course before in his BSc, but now it's in more depth. He'll be off soon to East Anglia and Yorkshire for a two week field course. There are also occasional day visits to a sand quarry in Leighton Buzzard and local trips, such as looking at gravel extraction and the River Loddon.

It will be 'mega thoughts time' from Easter to late August when he's writing his dissertation. This will be the 'Petrogenesis of cherts (flints) in the Portland Limestone Formation – Isle of Portland'. He has made a good start as he will be using material he already has and adding to it with photographs, samples and field sketches. Most of this work will be done on his own with some lab supervision. Stephen is enthusiastic about the laboratory equipment in the Allen Laboratory at Reading. The access to the computers is also very good. He uses the main library a lot – 'as we have a lot of extra reading due to the intensive nature of the course.'

'Life at Reading has been a contrast to my time at Portsmouth. I have gone from a student house at Portsmouth to a Hall at Reading. Postgraduate life can be more isolating than undergraduate life. We're a very small group here and the work load is heavy. There's not a lot of time to meet people, outside the course.' He tends to socialise with a small group from his course and, to get round the isolation factor, has joined the university conservation society.

So what of the future? The job market is still tough. Stephen feels that, 'Even at 23, I still don't know exactly what I want to do, but I've got a few interests. At the moment I'm looking for work overseas in Australia.' He will soon be tailoring his CV and writing letters. Environmental work is now a greater interest to him. He says that a lot of the work that is available is in oil and other mineral extraction industries, 'but you've still got to fight for it.' Later he'd like to do a PhD, funds permitting.

2. JONATHAN LESTOR, MA IN MORAL, LEGAL AND POLITICAL PHILOSOPHY

Jonathan has enjoyed philosophy for a long time and is full of enthusiasm. In RE lessons at school he began to feel that 'they said and argued for things that were not true.' This interest led to three years spent at Reading University on their BA Philosophy course, resulting in an upper second. He is now mid-way through Reading's new MA in Moral, Legal and Political Philosophy – a course that can be taken on a one year full time or two years part time basis. It is one of the three courses on offer in the department, along with an MA in Philosophy and an MA in Ancient and Modern Philosophy.

At the beginning of his third year Jonathan's thoughts turned towards an MA, and he filled in an application form. 'Because I was already a student here it was just a formality. It was despatched to the Philosophy Department, just for administrative purposes. I had already been told, "So long as you get the required grade, you're welcome", so it was all quite painless, though I was advised to think about other places as well.' Fellow students are a mixed bunch. There is one other student from his BA course; others include two Americans and a Serbian student who did not stay.

The key choices to be made on the course are between essays plus exams or essays with a dissertation. The taught time component gives Jonathan a choice from five options. 'I have to choose two, which means I have two lectures and a seminar each week. And there's lots of reading – as much time as someone might spend watching TV.' He reads constantly for a week, then his thoughts come together in an essay. 'I have to do two essays of 6,000 words per term per topic. This averages out at around three to four hours a day – say twenty hours a week extra work.' He feels that a master's course is harder than the first degree, although life is made easier by an excellent library. He feels that access in the library to books and information is about 70% successful. In addition, the department is very willing to provide books and articles, and philosophy reference material is also available on CD Rom.

Moving from undergraduate study to postgraduate study means that his relationship with the department is different. Jonathan says, 'There is ample chance to enter into philosophical debate with people who are a lot more experienced than you. You go from a little pond into a bigger pond.' He finds himself presenting a paper to academic staff and postgraduates, resulting in a discussion of his ideas.

It will be dissertation time in the summer. Jonathan has not yet decided on the subject. 'I am initially considering the political side, such as analysing the relationship between the individual and the state and also how nations are responsible for other nations. It has to be finished by 30 September and, as the course ends in early July, I will be spending the summer working at home adding the finishing touches.

As usual, there was no easy method of funding the course. Jonathan spoke to his local education authority who told him that it was illegal for them to support his course. Jonathan says, 'Everywhere you go they suggest a Career Development Loan. I didn't think it was really geared to MA students, but I had to take one.' He feels, 'It's hard to manage your money at university anyway, whether for undergraduate or postgraduate work.'

Staying on as a postgraduate in the same department has been ideal. 'One reason I stayed is because it's like adding another year to my degree. Also, there is excellent supervision here.' Staying in the same place meant that he already felt settled when he started his MA. He has spent all four years in hall, moving between two, and says that all halls accept postgraduate students. 'Overall', he says, 'if you really find the subject fascinating, the extra year really enhances your understanding and puts a gloss on the subject.'

So what next? Jonathan says, 'I've always had it in mind to do a PhD, but I've now got to earn some money, so it will have to wait for a while.' He has just seen a careers adviser – 'who was very encouraging about my qualities for being an employee.' He is also planning to use the computerised guidance systems available at the Careers Advisory Service. He'll be surveying the range of jobs open to graduates in any discipline.

By the end of term he hopes to have more idea about what he's applying for, in terms of immediate opportunities and long term ideas. And, he says, 'I'll have to juggle the two – finishing off the course and applying for jobs.' He has three months after the end of the course before paying back the career development loan becomes a reality.

3. RALPH BLANEY, PhD IN AGRICULTURAL ECONOMICS

Ralph has put a sign saying, 'Ralph Blaney works hard in here' on the door of his office in the Agricultural Economics Department at Reading University! He has certainly had to work hard and be persistent to have got this far. He started out with a degree in Agriculture with Agricultural Economics at Bangor University, obtaining an upper second. This was followed by an MSc in Agricultural Economics at Reading University. Now, after a year's gap, he has started a PhD, again at Reading University.

Ralph decided to take the postgraduate study route, having enjoyed working on his dissertation at Bangor. It took some organising. To get started he used the university careers service, and was helped by his tutor and friends. 'I did consider the jobs available in my field but was not interested in the management type jobs in agriculture and food.' He applied to several universities including Hull and Aberdeen as well as Reading. His choices were based on information from prospectuses and the opinions of staff and friends. However, getting financial support was the crucial factor. Ralph says, 'I really needed the funding – so it was a bit frustrating. In June, I knew I'd got a 2.1, but nothing lined up. I wondered if it was worth all the effort.' He says that some of his friends took out loans or were helped by their parents. In some cases universities waived the fees. Thankfully Reading University came through with the funding from the Ministry of Agriculture Fisheries and Food in mid summer.

So the year 93–94 was on spent on an MSc in Agricultural Economics at Reading. This involved around 16–20 hours taught time each week plus a lot of reading, essays and a dissertation of 12,000 words. Ralph chose to write about renewable energy on UK farms. 'The work was largely based around Reading University, apart from a few optional trips. Final results were based on exams. I felt that they were not a lot harder than the BSc. Looking back I would have appreciated more help with planning a dissertation, advice on research techniques, and more idea of the standard expected.'

Life socially has been a bit different as a postgraduate. The student mix was a bit of a culture shock because the majority of the class were overseas students in their 30s and 40s. However, Ralph says, 'It's interesting learning about different places without travelling.' He has also enjoyed life in the postgraduate wing of the hall of residence and likes the experience of the overseas students cooking their own dishes and speaking their own languages. The MAFF cash turned out to be just enough to survive on.

Ralph then had a year's break, which was not part of the master plan! He had applied to Cambridge and was accepted, but the funding from the Economic and Social Research Council did not materialise. He then applied to other universities for research assistant posts but was told he lacked experience. Employment opportunities in his home area, Cornwall, were also severely limited. Around January and February, he decided to apply for PhDs. 'It was a bit more difficult to find information as I didn't have the university facilities,' Ralph says, but he used reference material in libraries in Cornwall and wrote to MAFF about funding. Then applications were despatched to Exeter and Newcastle. He was interviewed at Exeter but without success. However, Exeter told him that there was a place at Reading, so it was back to his old territory for an interview. At the interview his previous studies were discussed. He felt that having had his bachelor's dissertation from his time at Bangor published was a great asset. Then there were questions about the topic of the PhD – 'Economics of Farm Animal Welfare.'

Ralph is now half way into the first of his three years. He is busy with lectures, seminars and essays and does a lot of his own research work in the university library. He feels the library facilities are good. He uses the computer facilities and has bought his own laptop. He also makes a lot of use of the Internet, and works late at night and at weekends to get access. 'The Internet gets busy when America wakes up!'

The money he has to survive on is about the same as in his MSc days.

Unfortunately, life is more expensive now as he has to stay all year round. His income will stay about the same over the three years but hall fees seem to go up more frequently. He carries out about two hours paid work each week for the department, helping on research projects. He will probably move out of hall next year, which will mean extra expense. Going to conferences will also be part of the PhD, but this will be covered by MAFF money.

Ralph feels it's important to plan his time sensibly – it's easy to take too much time off. It could be a lonely life, but it is up to the individual, and it helps being in hall and joining clubs. Overall, how his PhD develops depends a lot on his tutor. Ralph says, 'I am quite lucky as my tutor takes an active interest in what I am doing – not all do.' He feels there is more emphasis now on getting work published.

As to the future, Ralph started out thinking of research as his main choice of full time employment. Now he's finding out about the increasing trend towards short term contracts and he thinks he would prefer more stability. He says, 'I might look around for some government, European Union or United Nations type job or an aid agency.'

4. JANET HUGHES, POSTGRADUATE DIPLOMA IN VOCATIONAL GUIDANCE

Janet Hughes is busy juggling the demands of a full time postgraduate course in vocational guidance, her two primary school age children and family life. She is certainly achieving a lot, but it can be tough going at times. Janet is coming to the end of her second term on the one year Diploma in Vocational Guidance at Reading University.

She had a wide and very useful range of work experience behind her before embarking on this course, which trains future careers advisers, who mainly work for government funded careers services. Working life started after taking A levels at school, with a job in the Midland Bank in her home area of St Helens. Four and a half years later she moved on to work for the St Helens and Knowsley Health Authority, first as a statistics and information officer and then moving on to introducing a computerised system for general practitioners to record vaccinations and immunisations.

Then came the career break of six and a half years to look after her two children. It was back to work when she saw an advertisement for a project worker to carry out a feasibility study into setting up a parent support group for the local Chinese community. After a lot of hard work, the big day came when around a hundred Chinese people turned up for a community day. Janet was tremendously pleased with this as it represented over half the local Chinese population. She was based at St Helens College in student services and gradually became more involved with initial guidance for potential students, higher education admissions and selection of students.

Her thoughts had gradually been moving towards taking a formal qualification in vocational guidance. She had done an in-house RSA Certificate in Education and Training Guidance at the college, and a colleague had moved on to take a vocational guidance course at Manchester. Janet moved to Berkshire in April 95, so her application to Reading University seemed a natural progression. Along the way she had picked up the professional banking exams at work and an HNC in Business and Finance at St Helens College, so she was used to hard work. But, she says, 'If I was going to get another job, I was going to need this vocational guidance qualification.'

She got down to filling in the application form in February and says, 'I was bothered that I had left it too late.' This task really involved some serious thinking. The form included questions about the role of the careers adviser, but also the tricky ones such as, 'Working with people in a helping relationship requires self-knowledge and self assessment. Tell us something about your skills, qualities and what you know about yourself'; 'How do you think the course will add to your personal and professional development?'; and 'Tell us why we should invite you to a selection day.'

Janet obviously got it right because she was invited for an interview along with 15 others, who ranged from new graduates to 50 year olds. They were split into two groups and asked to discuss the topic, 'The Careers Service is free at the moment, but you are in a situation where you are going to have to charge. Discuss which clients you are going to charge and how to implement this policy.' During the 35 minute discussion the assessors where looking at the group dynamics.

This was followed by an individual interview with two people. Janet says, 'I was asked this awful question, "If you were a fly on the wall and there were two people who liked you and two people who didn't like you, what would they say?"' She dealt with it by talking about her strengths and weaknesses. There were other questions about equal opportunities and how she would deal with constructive criticism.

Janet must have said the right things because the offer of a place came through the same week. There are 21 students on the course, and she thinks there were at least 50 applicants. Fortunately Janet did well on the funding front. She says that points are awarded at the interview stage, and selected students are put forward by the university for Local Government Management Board awards. Initially there were only three awards available, one of which went to Janet. Fortunately, more money came through at Christmas for most of the other students. These awards cover the fees and pay £105 a week for living and other expenses. Two students have been sponsored on full salary by Surrey Careers Services. Those without this support have opted for Career Development Loans. There have been no local education authority awards. Another careers service has recently offered financial help, but requires the student to work for them should a job become available.

Janet's fellow students are from a wide range of backgrounds. Most are graduates, with a few having moved straight on from their first degree courses. One student worked in a bank before taking a degree and deciding on this course. Others have been in marketing, secretarial and training work. The course is a mixture of theory and practical work. Practical work so far has included a three week placement at Bracknell Careers Centre in Berkshire, where she observed a lot of the work done in local schools and looked at the structure of the Careers Service. Throughout the course there is also weekly interviewing practice in schools. She has just completed a week's industrial placement with Zeneca, and then there will be another spell with a careers service for three weeks in Warrington, where she will focus on adult guidance.

The theoretical side of the course covers topics like education, careers education and vocational choice theory. Janet feels that she is often having to cope with a heavy work load over a short period. It can be quite difficult fitting this around her family life, particularly when her husband is away. She says, 'I have to be quite single minded about getting university work done.' She feels a high level of motivation is needed to get through all the practical work. Fortunately everyone has survived so far! There are no exams, with the results based on assessments and completion of a work book.

The summer is approaching and three students have already got jobs. Janet needs a job in her home area and says, 'The job situation has been a bit thin locally, though it's OK if you're prepared to move.' However, this week there has been a new batch of advertisements from her local careers service. 'Given a choice I would like to work with adults again in a college or university setting.' However her first job will probably involve working with Year 11 pupils. Janet is obviously planning on a career in careers work, but she also feels that the skills she has gained would be useful for training, recruitment and selection.

5. STEPHANIE FOUNTAIN, PhD IN COMPUTER SCIENCE

Stephanie Fountain was naturally very pleased when she won a national computer science competition, the 'Softwright Innovation

Award' (with a prize of a £2,000 computer). The prize was for her final year BSc project on 'Optical Character Recognition for Hindi'. This was what encouraged her to think seriously about the possibility of research, although she had had this in mind for some time.

Stephanie took her first degree in computer science at Leeds University, finishing with a First. She's now in the first year of a PhD at Reading University which she started in October 1995. At the beginning of her third year at Leeds, she began to think about the future. She was not keen on the available jobs. She says, 'They all sounded very dull.' But she applied for one job because everyone else was making applications. She did look at MScs but would have wanted a research MSc and left it too late to get this organised. Looking back, Stephanie feels she should have started looking earlier, but she says, 'I was too wrapped up in my final year project to look. It's hard to do both.'

So she started to look at the PhD route. She could have stayed at Leeds but felt it was time for a change and wanted the opportunity to meet new people. She looked on the Internet for information about PhDs, and decided to target Reading, Manchester and Oxford. Around June the applications went off. Stephanie says, 'Reading got back to me the next day and it all happened in two to three days.' At the interview, her degree course work and the final year project were discussed. She decided to drop her applications to Oxford and Manchester.

Luckily the funding of her studies has been straightforward. Reading nominated her for one of their quota places, from the Engineering and Physical Sciences Research Council. So she gets her fees paid and receives £5,500 each year for living expenses. This will increase a little every year. Her cash flow is helped by the four hours' paid teaching per week that she has done this term. She is now dropping this in favour of a better option. She's been offered six hours a week consultancy by a computer company, to work on optical character recognition, which is related to her first degree project.

The company heard about her via the Computer Weekly magazine. She'll be working at home for one day a week on this project for three months. Then there will be reviews by the company to see that she's progressing and a discussion with the department to ensure she is not overdoing it. Stephanie says her fellow PhD students are also being paid for demonstrating, which involves helping with practical classes for first year students. Other students have got their main funding through the department, whilst one student is on a salary.

Stephanie is now six months into her PhD on 'Computer Vision'. She feels that there are not many companies currently operating in this field, but expects there to be more job opportunities when she finishes her three years of research. She points out that at postgraduate research level, there are no lectures and no deadlines and 'You' re left to it.' She didn't like it initially, and says 'I found it difficult to motivate myself at first.' She has to report to her supervisor every month, but at other times is working on her own. She is busy looking at other peoples' papers. For this she uses the Internet and on line data bases. Knowing what to look for can be a problem. There is a conference coming up in Edinburgh, for which submissions are due in at the end of April. She has to prepare a ten page report for this. She finds it helpful that this conference has given her a deadline to work to, and a reason to keep going. She will have to present a paper to an audience of a few hundred, made up of other postgraduate students, university lecturers and people from industry. The Engineering and Physical Sciences Research Council funds one conference and the university helps with others. Stephanie's hoping for an overseas trip, as most PhD students go abroad at least once.

Overall, Stephanie's made a smooth transition to life at Reading. She enjoys being in Reading as many computer companies are in the Thames valley, and likes being near London. She feels financially that it's better than as an undergraduate. She says that at Leeds, 'I unfortunately had to take out student loans.' She's living in a self catering hall on the edge of the campus, which is quite cheap. It's a sociable hall with a lot of foreign students, and she's enjoying the international atmosphere, and the experience of different cultures. There is a friendly atmosphere in the Computer Science Department, and she knows all the staff and other postgraduates. Her 'vision' group is made up of eight students and there are around 20 in total. Everyone is young and they have a social life together.

Stephanie has a further two and a half years' research. She's settled down well at Reading, but feels that this life only suits you 'if you don't mind being poor for three years.' It is also important, she says, 'to have your own ideas as you're not spoon fed any more.'

And what of the future? She's not interested in university teaching, and hopes to go into research with a company. She feels that by the end of her spell at Reading there should be more companies employing staff in her particular specialism. Heading north attracts her because she comes from York and would like to be near family and friends.

6. BRIDGET DUMPER, MA SCULPTURE

Bridget is a mature student – 46 years old, married with two sons aged twelve and fourteen years and an executive husband who travels all over the world.

She left school with a handful of O levels and went to work in a drawing office, where – 'I eventually became a leading draughtsperson in an office full of men – which was no mean feat. The company I worked for designed air conditioning systems.'

'At the age of 32 I started my family but decided I wanted, at the same time, to improve my qualifications. I attended a local college during the day time whilst my sons were in the college crèche. I studied for A level English and Art. From this I went on to take a Certificate in Fine Art at Eastleigh College of Further Education, near Winchester.' (At this time the family was living in Chandlers Ford in Hampshire.)

'By now, I knew that I was committed to art and that was where my future lay. I moved to Southampton Institute of Higher Education where I attended a part time diploma course studying painting and sculpture. Both my sons were at school by this time, which made attending college much easier. The course lasted for 5 years and I organised my time around family commitments.'

Although the diploma was of a recognised standard, Bridget felt very strongly that she wanted to study for a degree. This she did, gaining a place on the three year degree course in Fine Art at the Surrey Institute of Art and Design in Farnham. The daily travelling of 64 miles round trip was fairly demanding, particularly when her son had a major operation in her final year. Bridget thinks this affected her final degree class – a lower second rather that the anticipated upper second.

'During my diploma and degree courses I had carried out some part time teaching at Wyvern Community Centre in Fair Oak, Hampshire and Eastleigh College of Further Education. My classes were mostly adults, although I also ran some Saturday courses for children.

'By now we had moved to a village near the Hampshire/Wiltshire border. I was offered a place on the Post Graduate Certificate of Education Art & Design course at Reading University, but withdrew as I realised the journey each day would have been too gruelling.

'I felt that now was the time to consolidate my position and examine my motivation. My dilemma was that I enjoyed "making and doing" but I was also interested in the psychoanalytical position of woman in society. I therefore decided to undertake a two year part time research master's degree at Southampton University in Gender and Culture. My own particular emphasis was the history of women making art. I thought long and hard about teaching, as I knew it was something I enjoyed and would always be involved in. I came to the realisation that – for me – teaching would probably always support my art and not the other way round.'

After a year on the course Bridget realised that her interest did lie more in 'making and doing' and transferred to Winchester School of Art to take a one year full time MA in Sculpture.

'I work mainly in wood, metal and resin with lights and rubber being incorporated into my pieces. My work reflects very much what has happened, and what is happening, in my life. My feelings about women and the major influence they have on the world comes through in my sculptures.

The work load is very hard with very little respite. I usually start at college around 8.00 – 8.30 am and arrive home around 4.00 – 4.30 pm. I choose to work these hours as it means I am home to prepare an evening meal and to take part in family activities. Some evenings I work in the garage or, on occasion, carry on working at college.'

The emphasis throughout the course is on practical work. Each student has to present one seminar. Bridget chose 'Space' – which she illustrated with slides. Fellow students discuss and consider each presentation. These presentations happened fortnightly during the first term. In the Spring Term, each MA student was attached to a seminar group of BA students drawn from all three years. Once a fortnight they would spend a day with the group, leading a subject based analysis of their work. 'This is an exercise from which we all benefit and which we all enjoy.'

'One area in which the course exceeds my expectations is in the range and quality of visiting speakers, critics and lecturers. These outside speakers usually visit the course for an entire day and enter into dialogue with students in individual and group situations. These critics range from hard-core sculptors to minimalists to those with a conceptual outlook. They give each student a strong critical analysis of their work, which is invaluable.

'The school also runs central lectures for all MA students, which are informative and interesting. We had to present a mid-term show, which contributes to our overall assessment. The main assessment is at our end of year exhibition, which is put on at the school and then moves to London for two weeks. We have to find our own gallery, and the only written assessment is of our proposal for this exhibition. I have to say that standards are extremely high and we are constantly pushed to achieve excellence.

'There are five of us on the MA Sculpture course and I am the sole female and also the only one with a family. We are a very closely bonded group and integrate totally with all the other students. There is absolutely no division whatsoever between BA and MA students. We help each other set up pieces (as they can be big, heavy and unwieldy) and socialise together. As I have a family there are limitations on the amount of time I can spend "playing" with my fellow students but that, and that alone, is the hindrance to my joining in fully in social activities. Winchester School of Art has around 1,000 students, so is fairly small by today's standards. I think this helps with the friendly, sharing atmosphere. I must say that this contrasts greatly with the previous MA group I was involved with.'

Bridget does not have any financial problems but accepts that she is fortunate. Any art course can be expensive and sculptors work can be influenced by funds and what materials they can afford to buy and consequently work with. 'Some of my colleagues have, at times, had to rely on free materials. The only one of the five to receive a grant is a student from Greece and even he struggles financially.'

Facilities at Winchester are generally very good, Bridget says, but like every art course, space is at a premium. 'However, due to the timing of our course, we spend the last three months in the vast area usually reserved for BA students. As they finish their course at the end of June, we move in! Subsequently, we finish our course just as they return in September.'

'For some time I have been teaching fine art to a group of 7–13 year olds on a Saturday morning in a local private school. I thoroughly enjoy this as I like sharing the joy of art with others. I have been approached to teach part time on a foundation art course which I am very keen to do. I now see my future lying in lecturing at foundation and above level.'

7. LYN WILLIAMS, POSTGRADUATE CERTIFICATE IN EDUCATION

Lyn is married, 33 years old and has four children aged between two and nine years. Lyn's husband, Martin, was unfortunate to have his business fold about three years ago. Lyn, who comes originally from Sunderland, had gained her first degree, a BA in English Literature plus American Studies from King Alfred's College of Higher Education, Winchester in 1984. On graduating, Lyn worked for two years as a book buyer for W H Smith. She left to start her family.

Once the business closed, Lyn and her husband decided thay would make use of her degree and agreed that she should return to study whilst he looked after the home.

'Previously I had never wanted to teach, but helping out at my children's school had stimulated an interest in teaching which I now decided to pursue. I visited various schools and decided that I was more interested in teaching all subjects rather than specialising in one or two. Consequently I decided to train for primary school teaching.'

Having settled in Winchester made King Alfred's a logical choice for Lyn, but she was also more than happy to return to her old college as she felt familiarity would ease her return to study. Lyn obtained a place to start in September 1993 but discovered she was pregnant with her youngest child, so deferred the place. Lyn had applied through the Graduate Teacher Training Registry (GTTR) and unfortunately her deferment caused confusion as, when she reapplied, she was rejected. Lyn contacted King Alfred's, who rectified the situation, and her place was secured for entry in September 1995. Her selection had followed submission of her forms through GTTR and a 20 minute interview with the course leader. During the interview she was asked about her previous employment, interests and motivation for teaching. Lyn felt the interview was relaxed and informal yet quite searching and testing.

She says, 'I am thoroughly enjoying the course – in particular, teaching practices. There are lectures in the core and foundation subjects with all the other course members. Tutorial groups are arranged every week but there are no individual tutorials, although it is possible to sign up for individual discussions with a nominated special interest tutor. The course requires a lot of reading and I have to write three, 3,000 word assignments during the year. There are no final examinations.' Teaching practice is also assessed and so far Lyn has done very well obtaining 1's and 2's on her teaching practice reports.

Whilst on teaching practice, Lyn spends three to four hours each evening preparing her lessons, marking, report writing etc. This is obviously not easy with four young children around. 'It is not unknown for me to sit in the younger children's bedroom waiting for them to go to sleep, while attempting to write an essay, read a book or plan a lesson, by the light from the hall. Putting the children to bed is a ritual I am not prepared to sacrifice!' Whilst in college, Lyn is occupied five days per week from 9 am until 4 pm. 'The Autumn term was very heavy and I often ate my lunch on the run.' The Spring term was slightly easier – and to date no one has dropped out of the course.

Lyn found the course less frightening than she anticipated. 'I had been concerned about my ability to cope with returning to study, but I need not have worried. About two thirds of the students on the course are mature and this is extremely beneficial in terms of support, problem sharing and feelings of isolation in a predominantly younger environment.'

Finances are extremely difficult. Lyn is given a full grant and the family receives income support and other benefits. She has taken advantage of the student loan scheme but this went towards Christmas, school uniforms, school shoes etc. She has also received an Access grant from King Alfred's. Lyn and Martin are fed up with struggling financially, but both feel that the course and her future career are worth it. Martin does some part time work but obviously his time is limited.

The role reversal of Martin managing the home worked well at first, but the novelty is beginning to wear off. They plan that when Lyn starts teaching, Martin will increase the amount of work he does.

Lyn is aware that some people perceive her actions in a negative way, but this has added to her resolve to do well. She says, 'The course has increased my capacity to be more assertive and determined. This is an advantage because I feel that I was too "dithery" before the course. My role as a mother has proved very difficult at times though. I have missed out on my children's school assemblies and plays; dental appointments have had to be changed etc.' This is due to the fact that Lyn and Martin both feel that she should not be seen to be abdicating all her functions and duties, and Lyn wants very much to be there for her children. This causes added pressure and adds to the demands on her time.

Lyn wants to teach within the Winchester area, but it is a little early to have a definite job offer in place. She has sent some speculative letters to various schools and one has responded favourably. She is hoping to visit the school and meet with the head teacher soon.

She is concerned that the mention of four children may be off-putting to prospective employers, but – 'I am determined to succeed and I am working extremely hard at managing my time.'

8. PHILIP RICHARDSON, PhD IN LOW TEMPERATURE PHYSICS

Philip is in the last year of his research programme, at Royal Holloway College, University of London – which he went to straight from his first degree.

During the final year of his first degree in pure physics he took an optional course in two dimensional physics. This was a good step, he says, because it introduced him to his research field, and 'research is so specific that you must be really interested in your subject.' Unusually perhaps, Philip waited until he had his degree, an upper second, before making any applications. He did all the necessary research by himself, since he knew exactly what he wanted to do.

'I looked at all the universities doing research in this field, made a list and wrote to several, explaining what I wanted to do and enquiring about possibilities. I had replies from several, one of them from Mike Lea (Professor Michael Lea) who I was lucky to come across and who is now my supervisor. His letter said that he would be interested in receiving an application from me and invited me down to an interview. I came here, had the interview and was able to fit in time to look around the campus.' Because Philip's home is in Hull, the travelling time involved was lengthy and he could only stay at Royal Holloway for two hours. The interview itself was very relaxed, 'more of a discussion with Mike. He is very easy to talk to and enthusiastic about his subject. He also showed me round the department and I was able to talk to one of the postdoctoral researchers about the current experiments.'

Philip then had to complete an application form and submit a summary of his proposed research topic. Ultimately he was offered places by two other universities but accepted Royal Holloway because one of the others was for an applied PhD linked to nuclear

physics with industrial sponsorship and the other in X-ray crystallog-
raphy. He wanted pure research and so accepted Royal Holloway's
offer, which brought with it annual funding of £6,300 from the
Engineering and Physical Sciences Research Council.

Philip is in a research group of six people: Professor Lea, two postdoctoral researchers, a PhD from the Netherlands with them for six
months and two other students – one Algerian, the other Russian.
The team is conducting ongoing research into the magneto conduc-
tivity of two dimensional electrons on liquid helium. Philip has
joined then for the duration of his research programme. It is an international team and the research topic itself is being investigated internationally. 'There are groups working on this all over the world. A
European group meets every six to nine months to discuss and share
ideas. The seminars are held in one of seven cities where the groups
are based and I have attended ones in Eindhoven, Konstanz and
Grenoble. I'm due to go to Antwerp next and I shall also be attending the World Low Temperature Physics Conference in Prague.'

The research group work together as a team. It is a very different life,
Philip says, from that of his girlfriend who is doing a PhD in English
literature and works largely on her own. Team skills are extremely
important. They work together and decide in conjunction with each
other when to take holidays, which have to be arranged round experiments. 'When an experiment is running we can't take time off.'
Philip usually takes five or six weeks, although the official allowance
is eight. 'It's very important to be able to relate to one another. There
are some groups who don't – and it shows! It is also important that
everyone is interested and does their share. If you get one student
who doesn't pull his weight, it can be disastrous.'

In his first year, Philip's working hours were dictated by an experiment. 'Some are run on a 24 hour basis and need constant attention.
There were days when I was there for 14–16 hours.' Now he works
for more like eight hours a day, starting at about 9.30 or 10.30. 'But
there is no set routine. We are setting up a new experiment at the

moment so a lot of work is involved, but it varies from day to day. I often come in at the weekend. The lack of routine is one of the benefits. It never becomes monotonous.'

Philip meets his supervisor once a week – sometimes twice or three times. 'This is the way Mike likes to work. The six of us always meet as a group. We might be deciding whether to write a paper and who is going to do it – or we might interpret some data. We also give presentations to each other.' (Philip has already had three papers published in academic journals.) 'It is very different for my girlfriend who sees her supervisor once a month.'

The money he receives from the Research Council is 'just enough, if I'm careful. It covers accommodation, food and the occasional pair of shoes or jacket.' He lives on the campus in a postgraduate house and eats most of his main meals in the canteen. As Philip points out, he works irregular hours – and does not want to have to worry about shopping and cooking when he comes in. A main meal costs him about £3.00. Living where he does has made it easy to meet other postgraduates and to socialise outside his subject. He has also met undergraduates. 'At my former university undergrads and postgrads didn't mix. I don't know why that was. Here they do – through all the clubs and societies.'

Philip's thesis is due in at the end of the year. His funding also finishes then and he has to decide on his next step. He knows that he wants to stay in physics and in research. 'It would be a waste after all this time to go into something that doesn't specifically use my subject.' Having talked to postdoctoral research students who are enjoying their work, he has decided that he would like to continue in university-based research. Luckily, there are good opportunities in his field and he could apply for a contract in several countries, including Australia, Japan and the USA.

9. TOM PARKER, MSc IN THE GEOGRAPHY OF THIRD WORLD DEVELOPMENT

Tom is doing a taught master's course at Royal Holloway College, London University, where he also did his first degree – in geography – achieving a lower second. He decided on the course in his final undergraduate year because he was hoping to pursue a career in some form of environmental management. Added to that, he was keen to study aspects of the environment in more detail and found out that a master's course in his own department would give him what he wanted. He also knew from talking to people in his department that there was little hope of funding. So he made the deliberate decision to work for a year after graduating in order to save some money.

Tom did not make any applications in his last year. He asked when he should do so, and was told that there was no need to make an early application as he was going to be self-funded and would not be seeking any financial help. He then concentrated on getting his degree and finding a job. He found a job through an agency – working as a European customer services administrator for a computer monitor manufacturer. 'It was good for me', he says. 'Not only did I earn a salary but as the department I was in was small I also had a lot of responsibility and I made two business trips too.'

He applied for the master's course in February, giving two members of the department's staff as referees, and was accepted on the understanding that he would be paying for himself.

The year is not cheap. 'My fees are £2,500. Accommodation – I share a rented flat with a friend – takes £3,000 more and then I have general living expenses. I'm managing on the money I saved plus a Career Development Loan which I took out for £3,000. That will ultimately cost me about £4,500, repaid over five years.'

The course is hard work but enjoyable. Tom estimates that he works an average 40 hour week. 'The course leads to an MA or MSc depending on the options you take. I'm in the minority doing an MSc programme. Everyone takes a core course plus two options. I have chosen environmental processes and land management, and ecology and land management in tropical Latin America. There are two hours of courses for each every week. Because of one of my particular options I have to go to the Institute for Latin American studies in central London for one of them. That is interesting because I get to go into the centre, I meet different people and I can use London libraries while I am there.'

All Tom's teaching is done through seminars – of three students for one course; ten in the other two. Lecturers' styles differ however. 'One prefers to open up the discussion by talking to us and expecting us to join in at any point. Another gives us a reading list in advance and starts a discussion straight away.' He will be assessed through an examination in the core course and by submitting the two best essays of those he has to produce (ten of 2,500 words each over two terms). 'This means there is always an essay title in front of me'. In addition he must write a dissertation of 10,000 words. The outline had to be submitted in the first term, the first two chapters in the second and he will do the fieldwork in the summer.

'I have chosen to do an evaluation of land capability for agriculture. I'm going to Malawi for six weeks, where I can stay with a friend who is already working there. That will cut down on cost. I shall be restricting my research to quite a small area because of transport problems, but will be working in a very rural part of the country. When I come back I shall have eight weeks for the writing up. The dissertation has to be in by 13 September.'

Tom will continue to use the university's facilities during that period. They are good, he says. He has his own desk, drawers and filing cabinet in a room shared with 24 other postgraduates. (Work space is divided by screens.) There is access to a telephone, use of the photocopier is free and there is a dedicated postgraduate computer room.

What happens after September? 'I would like to get into either environmental management consultancy or making television documentaries. I realise this will mean starting at the bottom somewhere!' He has not made any job applications but is keeping an eye on advertisements in the press and on the Internet which 'has a good media jobs page. Some jobs are advertised in the department but are mainly academic posts. I shall start looking seriously when I get back from Malawi.'

Whatever happens in September, Tom would not have missed this year for anything. 'It has given me the chance to do something I really enjoy – and hopefully, will also lead to the type of job I want.'

10. LARIE MILLARD, MA CONTEMPORARY ENGLISH LITERATURE

Larie Millard aged 60 years in February 1997, is married and has two children who are grown up and have left home. Her husband is a self-employed builder and they live in Winchester.

Larie attended Winchester County High School, where she says she always felt out of her depth and did not do very well. The result was that 'I left school with four O levels in Art, English Language, English Literature and Religious Education and started what was perceived as a "good" job in local government.' Larie learned to type – a skill that proved useful in later life.

However, there was always something 'niggling at the back of her mind', a feeling that she could achieve more and had not fulfilled what she felt was her academic potential.

Larie feels that she pursued the 'normal route' for girls of her era – that is she did what was expected of her by other people. She left school, married and had her two children. While her children were very small, Larie stayed at home with them, but returned to work in a limited capacity as they started school. She started attending various evening classes, mostly for craft-type activities – pottery for example.

Larie can pinpoint the moment when everything changed for her. 'My road to Damascus was when I started a new job and someone told me there was no such word as can't', she says. So she enrolled for an academic evening class – O level history. This was in 1973/4 when Larie was 36 years old. After this, she studied English Literature A level and began to feel that she should go to King Alfred's College of Higher Education to study for a degree. Because Larie was working, running a home and bringing up a family, she studied the O and A levels over a period of several years.

Larie also studied for an Open University foundation course in social sciences but she felt restricted. 'The course was too dictatorial in what I had to read and there was no room for exploration.'

After a break from studying, Larie attended a Return to Study course at a local sixth form college. While on the course a visiting speaker encouraged students to apply for degree courses, so Larie decided 'to go for it'.

As a result, in 1987 Larie commenced a part time BA degree programme in History with English. The course was held on two evenings a week and took a long time. The result was that five years later, in 1992, Larie graduated with a 2.1 honours pass.

Larie's health had not been good so she took a three-year break. In October 1995 she began a part time MA in Contemporary English Literature. The course takes place at King Alfred's College of Higher Education in Winchester on one evening a week.

'The course is essentially student-led which I am thoroughly enjoying. There is a set course which is broken into components. The students each select a component – or topic – and lead a seminar on the subject. We have to present a ten minute paper and then to lead a discussion with the rest of the group. Tutors observe the seminars, make notes and bring out relevant points. The course is modular, so students can pace themselves over time. We have to submit a 4,000-word essay at the end of term with a final dissertation at the end of the course. There are no exams.

'In order to cope with home life and study, I have to organise my time to the nth degree. Hoovering and ironing provide great thinking time! I still work part time in the research Department of the County Council Planning Department.' Larie arranges her working life very well in that she works full time for one week followed by one week off. This system, she has found, fits in ideally with her studies.

Larie wishes that her qualifications could change her life more. However, she feels everything fits together very well as she lives eight minutes from work and ten minutes from college.

Although her family are very proud of her, Larie feels she has two separate lives – one at home and one at college. She thinks her family have difficulty identifying with her college work and rarely discuss her studies with her or read any of her work.

Larie's eight or nine peers at college are aged between 22 and 60 years and they get on 'amazingly well.' When in college they stay very much together and will go to the Students' Union for a drink, a cup of coffee or a chat. Some people on the course have dropped out for a variety of reasons. Larie does feel that as a group they usually stay on their own and do not integrate too well with other students in college. This is compounded by the fact that they are on an evening course.

One advantage to being an evening student is that the library and other resources are quieter. Larie thinks that the facilities at the college are good.

The course is proving to be quite expensive and Larie pays fees by monthly instalments of £53. At times she has carried out extra work to help pay for her studies. Having paid all this money for her qualifications, Larie would like to earn some money 'on the back of my MA in order to repay what it cost me – perhaps to help with or teach on an Access Course'.

16 SOURCES OF FURTHER INFORMATION

BOOKS

General

Higher Education in the UK. Research Opportunities

Higher Education in the UK. Taught Courses. Both from Pitman Publishing.

Postgraduate Study and Research. AGCAS careers information booklet. (Available from careers advisory services).

Guidelines. Booklets from the National Postgraduate Committee.

Postgrad, The Guide to Postgraduate Taught Courses and Research Opportunities in the UK. CRAC. Also on CD-ROM. An annual publication.

Surveys of Courses, AGCAS Vocational Courses Sub Committee. Individual surveys on vocational and professional courses. (Available from careers advisory services.)

Current Research in Britain. Volume 1 Physical Sciences; Volume 2 Biological Sciences; Volume 3 Social Sciences; Volume 4 Humanities. British Library. Annual publication.

MBAs

Guide to Business Schools , published by AMBA.

Directory (details of over 100 courses in the UK), published by ABS.

Which MBA? A Critical Guide to the World's Best Programmes, published by Economist Intelligence Unit.

How to Choose Your MBA Course, published by Trotman and Company 1997.

Overseas Opportunities

International Guide to Qualifications in Education, published by UK NARIC (care of the British Council).

Postgraduate Information Pack, Educational Advisory Service, the Fulbright Commission (USA).

Work and Study Abroad, AGCAS.

Guide to Postgraduate Study in Europe, FEDORA (Forum Européenne de l'Orientation Académique).

Higher Education in the European Community, Longman. Contains a chapter on the education system of each country together with cost of living information. Also has a chapter on the European University Institute in Florence.

Peterson's Guide to Graduate Programs, (USA).

International students coming to Britain

British University and College Courses, Trotman and Company.

Finance

Funding Body handbooks.

The Grants Register, Macmillan Press Ltd.

Educational Grants Directory, Fitzherbert and Eastwood.

Charities Digest, Family Welfare Association.

Directory of Grant Making Trusts, Charities Aid Foundation.

Students' Money Matters, Trotman and Company.

LEA Discretionary Awards for Postgraduate Courses, AGCAS Survey.

For Study Abroad

Awards for Postgraduate Study at Commonwealth Universities, Association of Commonwealth Universities.

Commonwealth Universities Yearbook, Association of Commonwealth Universities.

Scholarships Abroad, British Council.

Guide to Awards Open to British Graduate Students for Study in Canada, Canada House (Canadian High Commission).

Assistance for Students in Australia and the UK, Australia House (Australian High Commission).

Postgraduate Information Pack, Educational Advisory Service, the Fulbright Commission (USA).

International students coming to Britain

Sources of Assistance for Overseas Students, British Council.

Law students

Register Of Solicitors Employing Trainees (ROSET) includes information on firms offering sponsorship. (Available from careers advisory services.)

ADDRESSES

General

British Council
Medlock Street
Manchester M15 4PR
Tel. 0161 957 7193

Central Applications Board
P O Box 84
Guildford
Surrey GU3 1YX
Tel. 01483 451080

Graduate Teacher Training Registry
Fulton House
Jessop Avenue
Cheltenham
Glos GL50 3SH
Tel. 01242 225868

National Postgraduate Committee
General Secretary, Ewan Gillon
Department of Management and Social Science
Queen Margaret College
Clerwood Terrace
Edinburgh EH12 8TS
Tel. 0131 317 3629

The Open University
Walton Hall
Milton Keynes MK7 6AA
Tel. 01908 653808

Social Work Application System
Fulton House
Jessop Avenue
Cheltenham
Glos GL50 3SH
Tel. 01242 225977

MBAs

Association of Business Schools (ABS)
344/354 Gray's Inn Road
London WC1X 8BP

Association of Masters in Business Administration (AMBA)
15 Duncan Terrace
London N1 8BZ

Graduate Management Admissions Council
Educational Testing Service, PO Box 6108
Princeton NJ 08541–6103 USA

PasTest (for copy of the GMAT Information Bulletin)
Egerton House
Egerton Court
Parkgate Estate
Knutsford
Cheshire WA16 8DX

GRANTS

DfEE
Mowden Hall
Staindrop Road
Darlington
Co. Durham DL3 9BG
Tel. 01325 392803

Student Awards Agency for Scotland
Gyleview House
3 Redheughs Rigg
Edinburgh EH12 9HH
Tel. 0131 244 5847

Department of Education, Northern Ireland
Rathgael House
Balloo Road
Bangor
County Down BT19 7PR
Tel. 01247 279279

States of Jersey, Education Department
PO Box 142
Jersey JE4 8QJ
Tel. 01534 509800

States of Guernsey, States Education Council
Education Department
Grange Road
St Peter Port
Guernsey GY1 1RQ
Tel. 01481 710821

Isle of Man, Department of Education
Murray House
Mount Haverlock
Douglas
Isle of Man
Tel. 01624 685784

Funding organisations

Biotechnology and Biological Sciences Research Council (BBSRC)
Polaris House
North Star Avenue
Swindon SN2 1UH
Tel. 01793 413200

Economic and Social Research Council (ESRC)
Polaris House,
North Star Avenue
Swindon SN2 1UJ
Tel. 01793 413000

Engineering and Physical Sciences Research Council (EPSRC)
Postgraduate Training Services
Polaris House
North Star Avenue
Swindon SN2 1ET
Tel. 01793 444000

Medical Research Council (MRC)
20 Park Crescent
London W1N 4AL
Tel. 0171 636 5422

Natural Environment Research Council (NERC)
Awards and Training Section
Polaris House
North Star Avenue
Swindon SN2 1EU
Tel. 01793 411500

Particle Physics and Astronomy Research Council (PPARC)
Polaris House
North Star Avenue
Swindon SN2 1SZ
Tel. 01793 442000

Ministry of Agriculture Fisheries and Food
Nobel House
17 Smith Square
London SW1P 3JR
Tel. 0171 238 6000

The British Academy
Humanities Research Board
Block 1 Spur 15 Government Buildings
Honeypot Lane
Stanmore
Middlesex HA7 1AZ
Tel. 0181 951 5188

Central Council for Education and Training in Social Work (CCETSW)
Derbyshire House
St Chads St
London WC1H 8AD
Tel. 0171 278 2455

CCETSW
Wales Office
West Wing
St David's House
Wood Street
Cardiff CF1 1ES

Educational Grants Advisory Service
501–505 Kingsland Rd
Dalston
London E8 4EU
Tel. 0171 254 6251

For study overseas

Association of Commonwealth Universities
John Foster House
35 Gordon Square
London WC1 0PE

The Educational Advisory Service of the Fulbright Commission
62 Doughty Street
London WC1N 2LS

UK Committee for the College of Europe
UACES Secretariat
Kings College
Strand
London WC2R 2LS

For international students

British Council
Medlock Street
Manchester M15 4PR
Tel. 0161 957 7193

UKCOSA, The Council for International Students
9–17 St Albans Place
London N1 0NX
Tel. 0171 226 3762

Information may also be found on the Internet.